THE Culturally Inclusive Educator

THE Culturally Inclusive Educator

Preparing for a Multicultural World

DENA R. SAMUELS

Teachers College, Columbia University
New York and London

Published by Teachers College Press, 1234 Amsterdam Avenue, New York, NY 10027

Library of Congress Cataloging-in-Publication Data

Samuels, Dena R.
The culturally inclusive educator : preparing for a multicultural world / Dena R. Samuels.
pages cm
Includes bibliographical references and index.
ISBN 978-0-8077-5592-1 (pbk.)—ISBN 978-0-8077-5593-8 (hardcover)—ISBN 978-0-8077-7334-5 (ebook)
1. Multicultural education—United States. 2. Cultural pluralism—United States. 3. Minorities—Education (Higher)--United States. 4. Educational equalization—United States. I. Title.
LC1099.3.S36 2014
370.117—dc23

2014027975

ISBN 978-0-8077-5592-1 (paper)
ISBN 978-0-8077-5593-8 (hardcover)
ISBN 978-0-8077-7334-5 (ebook)

Printed on acid-free paper
Manufactured in the United States of America

21 20 19 18 17 16 15 14 8 7 6 5 4 3 2 1

To my best friend and ally, Steve,
an educational leader whose integrity and commitment
to his students and colleagues have always been an exemplar for me.

And to all the educators, administrators, counselors, and staff members
who enthusiastically encourage, engage, and empower one another and
especially ALL students to live, work, and create meaningful connections
in our growing multicultural world.

Contents

Introduction

Being an educator means being in the service of others. As an educator of many years, my ultimate goal is to connect with students. In whatever situations and environments we find ourselves, where we are summoned to teach, to lead, and to connect, we must know that we are being invited to a higher calling, a higher purpose. I don't mean this in a religious sense. Our awakening as teachers is rooted in the idea of connecting with others in order to deeply communicate: both listening to other people's ideas, perspectives, experiences, challenges, and sharing our own, regardless of the *actual* content of our teaching. We are invited to a shared experience where all involved are learners, including ourselves, and all involved have an opportunity to teach.

Students need that connection in order to learn. Without it, in isolation, they are less likely to persist in school, and their motivation can be severely compromised. All students need this connection to their teachers to succeed, and more, to soar inside the classroom and beyond. Unfortunately, based on socially constructed ideologies, stereotypes, and most important, lack of learning in this area, we often don't realize the ways in which we fall into these ideologies and stereotypes to the benefit of some students, and the exclusion of others.

This book challenges us as educators and administrators to wake up to what we need to learn to inspire *every* student to excel. As you will see, in general, we are not taught how to do this. Therefore, we have to take it upon ourselves to learn what we don't know we don't know. We must explore social identities (including our own) and analyze the impact that those identities have on our lives. We must reflect on the assumptions we have been taught to make about ourselves and others, figure out where those ideas came from, and determine whether they continue to serve us as educators. The goal of this book is not to suggest that there is such a thing as THE *Culturally Inclusive Educator,* but rather that as we grow in our teaching methods and relationships, we are forever striving toward inclusiveness —knowing that the end goal is constantly changing and illusive even as we continue to expand our knowledge and understanding of our differences.

Educational settings are a microcosm of society. They represent the diversity that is manifest in an increasingly multicultural world. The classroom can be our laboratory for learning how to engage and connect with one another across our social differences. In the future, our classrooms will look different from the way they look now. As we become more globally conscious, we become more aware of the differences between us. As technology soars, we can learn about one another and about diverse cultures through the touch of a few keystrokes. Students sitting in the classroom will be more versed in social differences, and they will expect their educators and administrators to keep up with a changing world.

In the future, who will be in our classrooms? Which social identities will be represented that we may not have considered before? For example, based on the recent sweeping reforms for gay rights, and specifically for gay marriage, it is more likely that there will be more students with openly gay parents and more students, faculty, and staff who are willing and able to come out as LGBTQ (lesbian, gay, bisexual, transgender, queer/questioning). Another example is the increase of veterans returning to college. Once shrouded in secrecy, more people in society in general, and veterans in particular, are open about posttraumatic stress and/or traumatic brain injuries from which they have suffered and/or continue to endure. And as physical access increases in all educational institutions due to reforms made by the disabilities movement/communities, we will welcome more members of the educational community who have physical disabilities.

In addition, more and more nontraditionally aged students are coming back to school to finish their education. We will continue to have a variety of generations in our classrooms. Further, as the wealth gap continues to grow, we will have more students living in poverty. And as we approach 2050, White people will become a numerical minority in the United States. The bottom line is, as our world becomes more and more multicultural, we will need to consider how these diverse identities and experiences will affect our classrooms and our learning and teaching environments. In our growing multicultural arena, it is critical that we are prepared to meet the needs of our constituents.

Unfortunately, most educators believe they are already prepared to build cultural inclusiveness in the classroom. Yet, how could they be prepared? Overwhelmingly, educators are not taught how to handle diversity and inclusiveness issues either in or outside of the classroom. This must change if we consider the facts from a student perspective:

- Schools with more students in poverty are more likely to have: teachers who are unlicensed in their subject area, higher student-teacher ratios, lower teacher salaries, and traditional, rather than

innovative, teaching methods and curricula (Oakes, Rogers, & Silver, 2004).
- Ninety percent of all public school teachers are White, and over 40% of schools do not employ a single teacher of color (National Collaborative on Diversity in the Teaching Force, 2004).

The Gay, Lesbian & Straight Education Network (GLSEN.org) reports:

- Ninety-seven percent of all students in public high schools regularly hear homophobic comments from peers. Worse still, 53% report hearing homophobic remarks from school staff or faculty!
- Ninety-three percent of transgender students report verbal harassment based on their sexual orientation, gender, or gender identity/expression. Unprotected by their educational institutions, 33% report assault.
- Lesbian, gay, bisexual, and transgender teens are twice as likely to consider suicide because of the way they are treated, three times as likely to create a suicide plan, and four times as likely to make a concerted suicide attempt.

These and other disturbing statistics indicate the critically important role we can play as educators, administrators, policymakers, counselors, paraprofessionals, and so on. These are concerns that alter one's standard of living at best, and one's life chances at worst. They demonstrate that we are not yet ready for the growing multicultural world that is emerging before us.

Our educational system and all of its stakeholders need to make a paradigm shift in thinking about how we educate our students. Too often, we rely on the old, tired methods of teaching to get our students through the system. The dominant ideologies have persisted and the consequence is that we are failing our students—there are too many who are dropping out, having been taught that they were not capable of succeeding in school.

If you look back at your own education, if any teacher stands out, it is likely to be the one (or two, if you're lucky) who used unorthodox methods of teaching, the one who made the classroom come alive with energy, excitement, creativity, and innovation. It is the one teacher who made you excited about going to school. Perhaps that teacher was a caregiver who inspired you to read or learn or follow your passion, the one who encouraged you to experiment or consider the world in a new light, to take on different perspectives you had never considered before.

My inspiration was a vibrant teaching assistant (TA) to whom I was assigned for my recitation section of a sociology class that I took my senior year of college. Although I thought I had received an outstanding liberal arts education up to that point, this TA opened my eyes to what I didn't know I had been missing. Although I had had teachers in my K–12 experience who had motivated me and made me feel more at home in the classroom than I did in my troubled household, this TA changed my perspective on life, and altered the trajectory of my career.

My TA incorporated transformative learning into her curriculum mostly by encouraging us to consider perspectives that were different from our own. Even as someone who then identified as an empowered White, heterosexual, gender-conforming female, I had never before learned about feminist theory, race theory, or queer theory. The TA encouraged us to consider our own social identities for the first time and how they impact our lives. I remember writing a paper on the idea of gay parenting for that course. I am embarrassed to say that it was a challenging concept for me at that time. What I remember most about this TA is that even as an *out* lesbian herself, she did not judge what I now consider to be a closed-minded perspective. She treated me with compassion instead, and that paved the way for an openness to new ideas that I could never have predicted. Had she judged me, I sincerely doubt that I would have dedicated my career and my life to social justice activism.

The idea of compassion in educational settings is not insignificant. We know that members of educational institutions are committed to the content they are teaching, but may not consider the hidden messages that may be threatening the well-being and safety of our students and colleagues. We know that students, faculty members, and administrators do not thrive if they are worrying about how they will be perceived when they walk into the building, or the extent to which they fit into a stereotype. These concerns not only stifle education and trample on creativity, but cause lifelong mental and physical health problems—even shortening one's life span. Is this the kind of educational environment we want for the 21st century?

The paradigm shift I am suggesting is rooted in the idea that every K–20 campus member deserves our attention, respect, and compassion. Students deserve to have their identities reflected in their educators and their course materials. The paradigm shift involves deeply reflecting on how our own social identities, life experiences, attitudes, and behaviors affect the lives of every student, faculty member, and administrator that we touch. Consider, if you will, the possibility that some of those attitudes and behaviors might, unintentionally, be including some members of our educational communities, and excluding others. I ask that we consider—really consider—whether we are prepared to motivate students of every race, gender, sexuality, age, and so forth? Are we aware of what we can do personally to make a difference in every school/campus member's life? This is not a simple question.

Using an interdisciplinary approach, this book assesses our current educational system and challenges us to consider the way we do our jobs. It asks that we consider what we could be doing differently on an individual level to engage and empower not just students, but also faculty, staff, administrators, and other K–20 stakeholders to create a welcoming, inclusive, exciting environment for the 21st century. As the global community becomes more interconnected and we are exposed more and more to different people with viewpoints that are different from our own, we need to be prepared, and we need to prepare our students.

This book begins with an overview of the challenges that members of the educational community face in terms of their willingness and ability to develop culturally inclusive environments. The concept of cultural inclusiveness is then grounded in a theoretical framework, which serves to combine theory and practice (praxis) to gain knowledge, understanding, and recommendations for the future. Chapter 2 provides a synopsis of a national quantitative research study I recently conducted on faculty preparedness to build cultural inclusiveness. Incidentally, faculty members believe they are prepared, but they still admit that they have not had the training necessary to behave inclusively. This leads us to Chapter 3, which provides a discussion of the benefits, challenges, and best practices of diversity training so that educators can actually become as prepared as they believe they are!

Chapter 4 considers a myriad of transformative strategies for building culturally inclusive classrooms and schools/campuses. Chapters 5 and 6 ask educators to look deeper at their own identities, beliefs, biases, and interactions with the intent that this reflective self-awareness can truly bring about concrete change. The book concludes with a discussion about cultural inclusiveness as leadership, because those who practice cultural inclusiveness become role models not only for students, but also for all other K–20 educators, activists, and practitioners. Although some of the research described in this book is based in the context of higher education, the strategies for building cultural inclusiveness can be applied to all educators of any subject.

The approach of this book is rooted in social construction theory (Allen, 2005; Burr, 2003; Frankenberg, 1993; Glenn, 1999; Lorber, 1994; Shotter, 1993; Smedley & Smedley, 2005). Based on the literature that shows that the meanings of social identities (race, gender, disability, and so on) are not necessarily inherent in one's genes or biology, social constructionism asserts that those meanings can change both over time and across cultures, and are contextualized within sociopolitical and historical circumstances. For example, who has been considered a member of which race has changed markedly over the course of the past century or two. The exact same person who would have been labeled "slave" in the national census of 1800 could have been labeled "mulatto" in the national census of 1920, "negro" in 1970, and "White and African American" in 2000. The consequences of these labels are significant for both life chances and standards of living. Although the various races are still characterized in our culture as biologically determined, science has virtually confirmed that categorizing people based purely on their superficial skin color is not accurate (Gould, 1996; Obach, 1999; Omi & Winant, 2009). A much better way of explaining skin color differences is geographic inheritance: in other words, where our ancestors originated, and how close that location is from the equator (Schwartz, 2001). A person's so-called race does not tell us anything about them other than that individual is more or less likely to have benefited from the sociopolitical circumstances of their birth.

It is beyond the purview of this text to deconstruct the changing meanings of each social identity in this way. It is important to highlight, though, that the approach is social constructionist and as such supports the notion that because the meanings given to social identities are constructed in culture, those meanings can be deconstructed and perceived differently. The hope is that once we are aware of our own biases and behavior that we have been systematically taught, we can consciously choose to act differently, to the benefit and the inclusion of all members of our educational institutions.

A note about the language used in this book. In the social justice arena, I believe that there are many concepts for which we do not yet have vocabulary, or at least commonly accepted vocabulary. Some transgender communities, for example, use the term *ze* rather than *she* or *he*, to avoid the overly simplistic two-gender binary. Another pronoun that is becoming more commonly used that also avoids the two-gender binary is *they*. Some will argue that using the terms (pronouns, for example) with which a particular individual identifies is too complicated; It's chalked up as political correctness. However, if social change is created by paying attention to our attitudes and behaviors, then it is important to keep in mind that language is rooted in the former, and impacts the latter. I have tried to be as inclusive in my language use as possible, including the use of the terms *they/their* throughout the book.

In the same vein, I have chosen not to use the term *minority* anywhere in this book to refer to a group of underrepresented, underserved, or marginalized people. The reason for this is threefold. First, being called a minority is disempowering. I first started thinking about this when one of my students of color made his own T-shirt that stated, "I am not a minority." His feeling was that the word went beyond numerical measurement; it made him feel like he didn't count as much as those in the majority. Out of respect for him, I stopped using the word as a replacement for the words *people of color*.

Second, when people hear the word *minority*, they most often think it refers only to race. And this is corroborated by the fact that when it is not used in the context of race, there is a descriptor attached: religious minority, sexual minority, and so forth. As you will see, this book takes an intersectional approach to issues of diversity and inclusiveness. Thus, using words that reduce the abundant social inequalities that exist in society down to one identity, albeit an important one, minimizes the problems we must face.

Finally, when the term *minority* is used, it tends to make the majority invisible, as though inequalities are of concern only to those who are marginalized by them. The scope of this book, on the contrary, includes everyone. However our race, gender, social class, age, sexuality, and other social identities impact our choices and our lives, we are all part of the system of inequalities that exist. Therefore, we all must be held accountable for finding solutions that bring equity to all, specifically in terms of education.

I would like to express my appreciation to several people who have been incredibly supportive of this writing endeavor.

This book is one small leaf on the tree planted long ago by the groundbreaking efforts of so many social justice activists and educators. I have had the wonderful opportunity to meet some of them personally; others I know only from their inspiring words and actions.

To Teachers College Press for their confidence in and encouragement of me, especially to Brian Ellerbeck. To editor extraordinaire, Tara Tomczyk. To Abby Ferber, Andrea Herrera, and my colleagues in the Women's and Ethnic Studies program at University of Colorado at Colorado Springs for their ongoing enthusiasm. To Eddie Moore, Jr., who continues to teach me how to build community. To Daryl Miller, whose life-altering discussions with me have inspired hope and determination. To my support team: Polly Fiedler, Susan Patkin, Rita Soller, and Gayle Preheim, for their consistent guidance and love; without them, this book would not have been written. To my children, Alex and Rachel, for their love and excitement about the project, especially as I completed each chapter! And to Steve, whose compassion and willingness to accept life-altering change has been an inspiration to many, including me.

CHAPTER 1

Are Educators Prepared for a Growing Multicultural Population?

> It is not our differences that divide us. It is our inability to recognize, accept, and celebrate those differences.
>
> —*Audre Lorde*

"You won't believe the racist comment my teacher made in class!"
"One of my classmates was raging against homosexuality in class, and the instructor said nothing!"
"To lessen the number of students in class, my instructor actually told anyone 'with ovaries' to stand up and leave!"

During more than a decade of my own teaching experiences, students have shared with me their horror stories of being in classrooms where a racist, sexist, or homophobic comment was made. Sometimes the comment was made by a student and the faculty member in the room did not challenge the comment, while other times the comment was actually made by a faculty member. In either case, students have left the classroom feeling unsupported, disempowered, and in fact, often excluded. Some cases were so offensive that the student felt they could not continue in the class, much less at the institution. And these instances of discrimination are not unique. Research shows that bias on campus occurs most often within the classroom (Marcus et al., 2003).

THE CHALLENGE AHEAD

If current trends continue, U.S. Census Bureau demographic projections indicate that by 2043, White people will no longer be the numerical majority in the United States (U.S. Census Bureau, 2012). Despite the fact that the United States is becoming more and more multicultural, most educators are given no training on how to handle issues of race, gender, class, sexuality, and so on that arise in the classroom. They are also given no strategies to educate students on these topics so they can learn to embrace differences rather than fear them. On campuses and in schools that are becoming more multicultural, educators' behavior toward other institutional members can create an unwelcoming, even hostile, environment.

As Justice Blackmun stated in his Supreme Court decision in *University of California v. Bakke* (1978) more than 30 years ago, "In order to get beyond racism, we must first take account of race. There is no other way" (para. 14). Today, students and faculty of color are still underrepresented in higher education (Bensimon, 2005; Davis, 2002; Swail, Redd, & Perna, 2003; Ward, 2006). This marginal status on college campuses clearly demonstrates a problem not only with regard to recruitment, but also retention of traditionally marginalized group members. Sometimes faculty members are the only consistent institutional contact a student has in a college or university setting, therefore, faculty members can have a great influence on students in terms of both retention and achievement. As a result, faculty members have a great responsibility to create and maintain an inclusive environment.

Even though scholars in the field of multicultural education have been clear on the need for campuses to create policies on both recruitment and retention of campus members of color (Bensimon & Malcolm, 2012; Hurtado, Milem, Clayton-Pedersen, & Allen, 1998; Kezar & Lester, 2009; Milem, Chang, & Antonio, 2005; Moreno, Smith, Clayton-Pedersen, Parker, & Teraguchi, 2006), diversity training on campuses is not widespread. Clewell and Ficklen (1986) argued that without the cultural sensitivity and support of existing students, faculty, and staff, any increases in recruitment are often diminished by even higher attrition rates. In other words, without a concerted effort on campuses and in schools to create an inclusive environment, it is difficult, if not impossible, to retain diverse institutional members.

As Howard (1999) noted in his book *We Can't Teach What We Don't Know*, most teachers in the United States today are White and have not been given the opportunity to understand how issues of inequality play out in their students' lives, much less their own lives. Moreover, Grant and Secada's (1990) investigation of teacher preparation for diversity led them to conclude that research on these topics has been consistently tangentialized and underfinanced. Teachers and other leaders must be trained in these vital areas, or they run the risk of perpetuating inequalities, often unknowingly. It is to our benefit both ethically and financially (Lockwood, 2007) to embrace differences and make each student feel empowered and included.

Recently, individual universities and educator programs have attempted to overcome the lack of preparedness to handle a multicultural classroom by incorporating multicultural education into the curriculum. Results, however, have been limited at best (McDonald, 2005). A few studies have been

*Learn to embrace differences or we perpetuate inequality.

conducted to ascertain whether teachers feel competent to consider diversity issues in their classrooms. In 2000, for example, the National Center for Education Statistics found that only 32% of teachers surveyed reported that they felt at all prepared to address the needs of students from diverse cultural backgrounds (Parsad, Lewis, Westat, & Greene, 2001). If colleges and universities, and specifically, faculty members, do not assess their own challenges with this issue, create a plan to confront those challenges, and reassess their initiatives, they run the risk of failing the increasingly multicultural population of this country that they presumably strive to serve.

This is not to say that faculty development around diversity and inclusiveness is not occurring on campuses. Many campuses are implementing campus climate surveys; however, these do not delve into the attitudes and practices of educators. Instead, they ask general questions about perceptions of how diverse the campus is and about the safety of students from traditionally marginalized groups. Not that these perceptions aren't important to study; rather, they usually garner only superficial information to a much deeper problem. Current research is woefully lacking on diversity and inclusiveness, yet how can we improve if we are unaware of our current status? Therefore, it is not enough to look only at campus climate or even at institutional policy on this issue, but also to consider those school and campus members who can directly affect the experiences of students and other institutional members.

WHY IS CULTURAL INCLUSIVENESS IMPORTANT?

Teacher educator leaders C. Bennett (1995) and Gay (2000) stress that in order to be effective educators, teachers must furnish an environment that "adequately addresses student needs, validates diverse cultures, and advocates equitable access to educational opportunity for all" (E. L. Brown, 2004b, p. 325). In other words, culturally inclusive practices are critical to foster the retention of diverse students. Moreover, Sanders (1998) and Sanders and Horn (1998) conclude that teacher quality impacts student achievement more than any other factor, including socioeconomic status and family background, among others. Thus, teacher preparedness for building cultural inclusiveness impacts student achievement as well as retention.

Because educators have the potential to set the tone for their students' experience, it is important that we take account of faculty members' attitudes and behaviors in and out of the classroom. Further, how do their own social identities, biases, and intentions impact their willingness and ability to build an inclusive environment? Finally, the intersectionality of their social identities (i.e., race, gender, sexual orientation, physical ability, and so

* culturally inclusive practices are critical/impact students.

on) complicates the issue of preparedness, creating a more complex analysis and, therefore, a more thorough understanding of the challenges of creating inclusiveness. Before exploring educators' social identities and attitudes, we must understand everyday threats to inclusiveness, which will give us a clearer sense of what we're up against.

HOW DOES EXCLUSION HAPPEN?

Based on research that spans the topics of colorblindness (Bonilla-Silva, 2003), stereotype threat (Steele, 2010), implicit bias (Banaji & Greenwald, 2013), and microaggressions (Sue, 2010), it is clear that the challenges to inclusiveness are many. We can begin with Tatum (2003), who suggests that U.S. society considers talking about social identities, and race in particular, a taboo. Often, parents and teachers are afraid of being considered racist, so they think any mention of a person's race is off-limits. They teach this to their inquisitive children and students by silencing them or ignoring the topic altogether. As Tatum pointed out, "Their questions don't go away, they just go unasked" (p. 36), and it is often left to the child to fill in the blanks.

This situation prompted a timely study by Birgitte Vittrup at the Children's Research Lab at the University of Texas, the results of which were spotlighted in *Newsweek* (September 14, 2009). The study first asked White children between the ages of 5 and 7 from approximately 100 different families about racial attitudes. Then, it asked White parents to use a checklist to discuss various aspects of race with their children every night for 5 nights. The study found that parents were, at best, uncomfortable discussing issues of race with their children, and at worst, the parents outright refused to do so. A few of those who repudiated the study and dropped out responded, "We don't want to have these conversations with our child. We don't want to point our skin color" (Bronson & Merryman, 2009). The authors of the article point out that these parents did not want to call attention to racial differences, but rather that they wanted to have their children grow up colorblind. The pretest that was given to the children, however, showed that they did, in fact, see racial differences, despite their parents' attempts to affirm ambiguous principles such as "everyone's equal."

If parents and children are not taught to discuss these issues in a relatively comfortable environment, they are not likely to be prepared to discuss them in the classroom. By the time some of these White children grow up to become teachers, they are likely to have bought into the "everyone's equal" ideology and believe that it will be perceived as racist if they even mention race. Moreover, the mental gymnastics one has to do to avoid talking about race can severely impact encounters with others.

Colorblindness/Oppression-Blindness/Identity-Blindness

Colorblindness, also known as oppression-blindness (Ferber, 2007) or identity-blindness, is rampant in U.S. society. Scholars argue that ignoring our differences discounts those differences, disregards systemic inequalities, and is another form of racism (Bonilla-Silva, 2009; Gallagher, 2009). In fact, Bonilla-Silva (2009) called this relatively new form of racism *colorblind* racism. In the past, racism was overt, whereas this colorblind racism is covert. Outwardly, people say that they do not discriminate, that they are "colorblind." Their actions, however, demonstrate discriminatory behavior. Blaming the opportunity gap on students of color rather than their inadequate education (Love, 2004), red-shirting students of color (holding them back so their assumed inferior scores are not reflected on a school's Adequate Yearly Progress [AYP] scores) (Hong & Youngs, 2008), or tracking them into special-needs classes would be examples of this new covert form of racism in the educational system.

Oppression-blindness is even more insidious in terms of challenging inclusivity. This approach fits in with the culturally perpetuated myths of meritocracy, individualism, and equality: that if we all just work hard enough, we will succeed, no matter one's circumstances, race, gender, ethnicity, social class, and so forth. It assumes that we all start out on a level playing field, which not only ignores social structural inequalities, but also invalidates individual differences, claiming that being "American" is one overarching identity to which one can, and should, adhere. Those individuals in dominant categories are more likely to subscribe to the oppression-blind approach because it is more inclusive of their own groups. As a result, they are also more likely to identify more strongly with an oppression-blind organization, taking on the organization's broader identity and culture as their own (Dutton, Dukerich, & Harquail, 1994; Plaut, Sanchez-Burks, Buffardi, & Stevens, 2007).

Meanwhile, members of traditionally marginalized groups tend to consider colorblindness exclusionary (Markus, Steele, & Steele, 2000). In addition, this approach is correlated with higher degrees of racial bias (Richeson & Nussbaum, 2004), and may in fact alienate nondominant group members (Bonilla-Silva, 2003). Through a colorblind lens, as individual differences are minimized and even discouraged, so too are potential innovative, culturally specific methods of problem solving (Stevens, Plaut, & Sanchez-Burks, 2008).

Colorblindness goes even further. Many White Americans believe that if they pretend not to see a person's race, then they cannot be racist. They also believe that racism has been overcome. Gallagher (2009) cited national polling data to demonstrate that "a majority of whites now believe discrimination against racial minorities no longer exists" (p. 548). And in a recent study, coauthors from Tufts University and Harvard University found that contrary to the reality of racism, White people believe that racism against African Americans has decreased, but at White people's expense, Moreover, they believe that Whites are now the new victims of discrimination: that anti-White bias is a more significant problem in society than anti-Black bias (Norton & Sommers, 2011).

In addition, a 2013 Pew Research Center poll showed that only 44% of Whites agreed that the United States has a long way to go before reaching racial equality; almost 80% of African Americans believe this to be true. Moreover, only 15% of Whites agree that in their local public schools, Black people are treated less fairly than Whites; in contrast, 51% of African Americans agree with this assertion. Kiefer and Kraft (2003) found that 81% of White people believe that Black children have equal educational opportunities. Interestingly, since 1995, Gallup poll data show that White people's responses on this issue have remained relatively stable. Black people, however, do not share the same belief. Black people's opinion that Black children have educational opportunities equal to those of White children has actually dropped from 64% to 50% since 1995. In other words, Blacks believe that educational equity is worsening.

Kiefer and Kraft argue that Black Americans' concerns about educational opportunities for Black children are justified. It is more likely that Black children, compared with White children, will attend school in urban, as opposed to suburban, settings. Urban schools tend to receive less funding per student, and have more trouble recruiting and retaining qualified teachers (Flores, 2007; Kiefer & Kraft, 2003). In a quantitative study, Cameron and Heckman (2001) found that racial disparities in college attendance were due to the long-term financial constraints of the family. Given that even after the recession of 2007–2009, on average, White families have nearly 20 times the wealth of the average Black and Latino families (Shapiro, Meschede, & Osoro, 2013), it is clear that economic disparities between White families and families of color have significant consequences for the educational opportunities of those households.

Given the reality of racial inequality, the discrepancy in the perceptions of White people and Black people regarding educational equity highlights the inability of White people to acknowledge the racial inequalities that exist in the U.S. educational system, most likely due to colorblindness (Gallagher, 2009). And this makes sense. If White people have been taught to ignore race and not confront their own learned racism, then they are not likely to see it or consider it a problem. They would have to be educated that it is, in fact, a problem. Moreover, if people, and teachers especially, do not perceive that a problem exists, they are not likely to seek solutions in the educational system, or within themselves.

Stereotype Threat

Stereotype threat emerges when a person feels at risk of being considered the stereotype that surrounds one or more of their social identities (Steele & Aronson, 1995). Steele (2010) describes it as a situation in which "one false move could cause [a person] to be reduced to that stereotype, to be seen and treated in terms of it" (p. 7). More than 300 experiments on stereotype threat have been published in academic journals (Nguyen & Ryan, 2008). Findings show that stereotype threat negatively impacts academic performance, whether the threat is based on race, gender, social class, or other social identities. Students who are being challenged by a stereotype put substantial amounts of mental energy into being vigilant about whether or not they are feeding into or countering the stereotype. This leads to a reduced availability of cognitive resources for the task at hand (Steele, 2010), and can result in a self-fulfilling prophecy of lower performance. For example, after watching TV commercials with women depicted as "ditzy blondes," female students scored 38% lower on math tests (Davies, Spencer, Quinn, & Gerhardstein, 2002). In another study, Steele and Aronson (1995) found that for African Americans, simply indicating their race prior to taking a test was enough to activate the stereotype threat, causing them to underperform. Stereotype threat has even been shown to lead women to demonstrate less interest in leadership roles (Davies, Spencer, & Steele, 2005), and to lessen career choices for those who are targeted by stereotypes (Schmader, Johns, & Barquissau, 2004).

On the other hand, Massey, Charles, Lundy, and Fischer (2002) found that stereotype threat based on race is alleviated by the presence of faculty (and other students) of color. Critical mass of traditionally underrepresented group members can make an otherwise exclusive classroom, inclusive. Other studies have shown that removing a negative stereotype can increase the performance of stigmatized individuals (Davies et al., 2002). Further, Davies et al. (2005) found that stereotype threat can be eliminated when the stereotype is openly challenged. For example, they created what they refer to as an "identity-safe environment" for one experiment group by including the phrase, "our research has revealed absolutely no gender differences ... on this particular task" (p. 281). The simple addition of this sentence mediated the stereotype threat that had been activated from a negative gender stereotype. In other words, it is possible to eliminate the effects of stereotype threat, contributing to the development of an inclusive environment.

This concept is demonstrated by Jane Elliott's groundbreaking experiment, depicted in the film *Eye of the Storm* (Peters, 1970). On the day after Martin Luther King, Jr., was assassinated, Elliott decided to do an experiment that might teach the students what it felt like to be discriminated against. She divided her 4th-grade class based on eye color and told them that the blue-eyed students were superior to the brown-eyed students. She then tested the students with flashcards. The following day, she told her students that she had been wrong the day before: that it was really the brown-eyed students who were superior to the blue-eyed students. She tested them again with flashcards. On the day the brown-eyed students were told they were inferior, it took them 5.5 minutes to get through the deck. On the day they were told they were superior, it took them only 2.5 minutes. It was faster than any group of students had gone in her class prior to that day. As Elliott states in the film, "The only thing that had changed was that now they were superior people."

Elliott comments in an ABC interview (StosselClassroom, 2009), "I set  them up to fail and they failed. If you aren't aware, you'll let it happen and you'll take that in and it will become part of your psyche. You don't have to take it in. It's time to kill the stereotypes." And she adds, "I had no idea that you could change a child's academic performance. When you're told you're superior, you act up to that. . . ." Elliott provides an apropos example of how, when educators are aware of this, they can provide cues that can make a big difference in student performance.

Implicit Bias

Whereas explicit bias is overt discrimination against members of a particular social group, implicit bias is covert, unconscious prejudice against a particular social group (Sue, 2010). Unfortunately, research shows that implicit bias is more challenging to change than explicit bias (Sue et al., 2007). Boysen and Vogel (2009) found that teachers were about half as likely to take action against implicit bias as explicit bias (e.g., stereotyping of a specific group). The authors concluded that many occurrences of bias tend to go unnoticed.

One of the ways social psychologists have found to test a subject's implicit bias is by using the Implicit Association Test (IAT). The IAT measures attitudes and prejudices toward specific groups based on various social group memberships (race, gender, age, sexual orientation, and so on) and is available on the Internet. The test asks respondents to quickly categorize words or images as positive or negative by the click of one or another letter on the keyboard (Greenwald, McGhee, & Schwartz, 1998). In empirical studies, McConnell and Leibold (2001), among others, found that discriminatory behavior correlated with more prejudiced IAT scores, demonstrating the validity of the IAT as a tool to predict behavior.

Devine (2001) suggests that implicit bias can be mediated by situational circumstances. Powell (2012) asserts that our ideas and associations can be affected by the way we frame them. This is known as "priming." That is, providing counter-stereotypic information before engaging with someone who has been targeted by that stereotype can reduce bias. For example, when participants were asked to simply conjure a mental image that challenged a stereotype (e.g., a strong woman), Blair, Ma, and Lenton (2001) found that they were subsequently less likely to stereotype women as weak. This study has implications for the malleability of prejudice and the relative ease with which one can challenge bias. Moreover, more exposure to a marginalized group tends to lead to less bias, suggesting that more intergroup contact, and specifically, intergroup friendships, can aid in overcoming bias (Aberson, Shoemaker, & Tomolillo, 2004). These and other findings submit that if educators are given the opportunity to learn about their implicit, and often consciously unintended, biases, then they can learn to challenge those prejudices before they act on them.

Microaggressions

Offensive comments or behaviors are known today as *microaggressions*. Racial microaggressions are "brief and commonplace daily verbal, behavioral, and environmental indignities, whether intentional or unintentional, that communicate hostile, derogatory, or negative racial slights and insults to the target person or group" (Sue et al., 2007, p. 273). Examples are abundant in the literature from the perspectives of students of color. They include, among others: faculty making assumptions about the intelligence of students of color; ignoring, distorting, or stereotyping the experiences of people of color; and racial segregation of students in study/work groups (Solórzano, Ceja, & Yosso, 2000). In their study, Solórzano et al. found that African American students felt "'drained' by the intense scrutiny their everyday actions received in the context of negative preconceived notions about African Americans" (p. 67). Moreover, these discriminatory behaviors are not just prevalent in colleges and universities; the literature shows they start much earlier, in K–12 classrooms, and are perpetuated not only toward African American students, but also toward other students of color (Ramirez & Carpenter, 2005; Schneider, Martinez, & Owens, 2006).

Further, Kottler and Englar-Carlson (2009) made it clear that microaggressions do not occur only around issues of race, but also around gender, class, age, sexual orientation, religion, and so forth. We can break microaggressions down into three basic parts: intent, underlying messages, and impact (Sue, 2010). First, it is unlikely that when people commit microaggressions against another person or a group of people that they mean to purposely insult or harm them. Mostly, microaggressions are the manifestations of stereotypes in the culture that are continually perpetuated through jokes, comments, and behavior. They often go unnoticed and, so, unchallenged.

When people are confronted on a microaggression, typically, they can easily brush it off by saying, "I didn't mean it that way." And if the confronter does not pursue the topic, the situation is over.

Unfortunately, these common, subtle barbs, which are rarely challenged, are engorged with meaning. They usually transmit a rather unwelcoming message. One example is when a person with a biracial or multiracial background gets asked, "Where are you from?" When the response is somewhere in the United States, the microaggressor replies, "No, where are you *really* from?" The intent here is either to get to know the microaggressee or for the microaggressor to ascertain if they had guessed correctly. The underlying message is that what it means to be American is to be White, and further, that this non-White person can't possibly be American.

The most important aspect of microaggressions to consider is their impact on those who are targeted by them (and their allies). Microaggressions lead to a rise in levels of cortisol (the stress hormone), and over time, this can cause mental and physical health problems, and even an increase in mortality rates (Sue, 2010). At the very least, in the classroom, microaggressions can trigger frustration, leading to feelings of marginalization and exclusion (Franklin, 1999; Pierce, 1988; Sue, Capodilupo, & Holder, 2008). When looked at more broadly, students who are the targets of microaggressions may not even be getting an equitable education, compared with those who are not targets. Moreover, considering that a common goal of many colleges and universities in the past few decades has been to recruit, retain, and support a diverse student body, it is imperative for faculty to reflect on their own assumptions and actions so as to eliminate, or at least minimize, the microaggressions that they may, unknowingly, be perpetuating. Dealing with these biases and subtle forms of discrimination is a topic that will be discussed in great detail in Chapter 5.

For now, we will turn our attention to a research study that will provide insight into how prepared we are for building cultural inclusiveness. Scholars suggest that in order for educators to become more culturally inclusive in our attitudes and behaviors, we must explore our own perceptions, attitudes, and experiences to uncover how they affect our behavior and our motivation to make a difference (Banks, 1995; Cochran-Smith, 1995b; Fried, 1993; Lehman, 1993; R. J. Martin, 1991). Thus, these are the dimensions of educator preparedness that will be explored.

THEORETICAL FRAMEWORK

Bridging theory, research, and practice, we can uncover how prepared faculty members are for a growing multicultural society. In particular, Critical Race Theory (CRT) (Ladson-Billings & Tate, 1995; Parker & Lynn, 2002;

Solórzano, 1998; Taylor, 1998) focuses on several axes of oppression, challenges current cultural ideologies such as White supremacy, is dedicated to social justice, emphasizes experiential knowledge, and makes use of an interdisciplinary perspective. In addition, Privilege Theory (McIntosh, 1988) is critical for explaining the ways in which systemic inequalities might be maintained and perpetuated. This theory calls for self-reflection on one's own social group memberships to ascertain the impact of these identities on our behavior. Further, Social Identity Development theory (Atkinson, Morten, & Sue, 1983; Cross, 1978; Hardiman & Jackson, 1997; Helms, 1984, 1995; Sue, 1981) is utilized to help explain the attitudes of faculty members. These development models provide a rough gauge as to where in the process faculty members might be currently, and can support their progress toward a more multicultural and inclusive outlook.

Critical Race Theory

Critical Race Theory (CRT) focuses on race as a way of understanding the social inequalities that exist in society (Taylor, 1998). Specifically, racism is deeply ingrained in our social institutions, which benefits some people at the expense of others (Parker & Lynn, 2002). CRT posits that experience and even reality is socially constructed. The theory paves the way for reality to be constructed differently (Ladson-Billings & Tate, 1995). CRT encompasses five aspects: (1) a focus on race and other axes of oppression (gender, sexual orientation, and so on); (2) a challenge to White supremacy and other dominant statuses (male, heterosexual, and so forth) as the current cultural ideology; (3) a dedication to social justice; (4) a focus on experiential knowledge; and (5) an interdisciplinary perspective rooted in ethnic studies, women's studies, sociology, history, and the law (Solórzano, 1998).

All five aspects of CRT work together to provide not only a basis for challenging dominant culture, but also a direction for creating a more inclusive educational environment for all. First, framing the challenge to current cultural pedagogies using an intersectional lens broadens the analysis beyond racism to include sexism, heterosexism, and classism, among others, in the curriculum.

Second, challenging dominant ideologies allows students with traditionally marginalized social group memberships as well as students with dominant social group memberships to expand their understanding of the world. It also prepares them for a growing multicultural society where they will need to create relationships with people who have different perspectives from their own.

Third, social justice is at the root of culturally inclusive environments. Bell (1997) defined social justice as the "full and equal participation of all groups in a society that is mutually shaped to meet their needs" (p. 3). She continued, "Social justice involves social actors who have a sense of their own agency as well as a sense of social responsibility toward and with others and the society as a whole" (p. 3). In this case, the social actors to which Bell refers can be both the educator and the student and their commitment to "full and equal participation of all groups."

Fourth, experiential knowledge is critical to classroom inclusiveness. Solórzano (1998) explained: "Critical race theory recognizes that the experiential knowledge of women and men of color is legitimate, appropriate, and critical to understanding, analyzing, and teaching about racial subordination in the field of education" (p. 122). This type of knowledge acquisition allows for diverse ways of learning, once again, broadening the scope of education beyond learning by rote. Moreover, experiential learning provides the opportunity for students from diverse groups to work together on projects, sharing diverse perspectives and experiences with other students.

Finally, an inclusive classroom brings together ideas and pedagogies, both theoretical and practical, that draw from many disciplines, including women's studies, ethnic studies, sociology, psychology, education, political science, and health sciences. Overall, CRT informs cultural inclusiveness both in terms of purpose and prescription.

Privilege Theory

Privilege Theory helps us understand the ways that systemic inequalities are maintained and perpetuated. In her seminal work, McIntosh (1988) depicted privilege as the "unearned benefits" that one social group is given at the expense of another group based on social group memberships (race, gender, sexual orientation, and so on). Hill Collins (1990) expanded on McIntosh's work and focused on the intersections of individuals' identities and the ways in which some of our statuses can benefit us while others can serve to disadvantage us. In other words, privilege exists when one group is afforded access to resources, opportunities, legal rights and protections, and notions of societal belonging and acceptance that others are denied because of their status as members of another social group (Johnson, 2006). It is important to note that everyone is endowed with *some* type of privilege in society, whether it is based on their heterosexuality, mental ability, male gender, Christianity, and so forth. The ways in which we are privileged affects our life chances, the impressions we make on others, and our own sense of identity (Ferber, Jiménez, O'Reilly Herrera, & Samuels, 2009).

One way I like to think about the concept of privilege is to consider that you are swimming in jellyfish-infested waters. You don't see the jellyfish because they tend to be translucent, but you know they are there. If we use the analogy that each jellyfish represents systemic forms of oppression such as racism, sexism, heterosexism, ableism, and classism, with long tentacles that produce a wallop when they come into contact with human beings, then having privileged identities is comparable to swimming through those waters in a wetsuit: buffered against the threat of attack.

Just as with oppression and discrimination, being affected by one disadvantaged identity is the equivalent of being stung by one jellyfish. However, if you were affected by more disadvantaged identities, you might not survive the onslaught of tentacles. Moreover, you would likely spend more of your time healing from past wounds and bolstering yourself for the next attack than having the luxury of enjoying the swim. The wetsuit provides not only protection from the jellyfish (systemic forms of oppression), but also has the added benefit of the comfort of warmth in the cold water. Entitlement enters into the equation when those who have a wetsuit assume that everyone has one, and if they don't, it's due to their personal shortcomings rather than systemic inequality. Further, some of those who don't have the privilege of a wetsuit may at least have some access (i.e., privilege/status) to health care to help them heal, while others do not.

What is critical to point out is the invisibility of privilege and the ways in which dominant statuses are considered the *norm* (Johnson, 2006). When privilege is normalized, those in dominant positions tend *not* to see themselves as privileged, and run the risk of ignoring their own role in perpetuating inequalities. In fact, Powell, Branscombe, and Schmitt (2005) suggested that framing social inequalities only in the context of the disadvantaged "outgroup" encourages prejudicial attitudes by privileged group members. Thus, framing the problems of campus inequalities only in terms of those who belong to disadvantaged social groups could lead to a biased understanding of the problems, and therefore, to biased solutions. In other words, educators and institutions might "blame the victim" for their failure to apply to college or to remain there once accepted, rather than reflecting on their own role in perpetuating an exclusive environment. On the other hand, if we can incorporate the concept of privilege into the framework for understanding these inequalities, we might uncover previously hidden biases, which will enable us to create more equitable solutions.

Finally, as has been stated previously, outgroup members are more likely to feel marginalized, ignored, and/or excluded on campus. What is often missing from the equation is how those who belong to privileged categories, in contrast, systematically feel *included* on campus. The invisibility of privilege allows those with privileged statuses not to have to ask this question, as though it were irrelevant to the problems of inequality.

There is an inherent connection between privilege/oppression and inclusion/exclusion. It is often the case that those who belong to privileged social groups in a given context do not realize that their attitudes and behaviors may be exclusionary toward underrepresented group members. Further, what is often missing is a self-reflective understanding of an educator's own role/collusion in the systemic power inequalities that work to privilege/include dominant statuses (e.g., White, male, wealthy) at the expense/exclusion of others (e.g., people of color, women, poor). Plantenga (2004) suggested that the goal for transformative diversity training is to acknowledge these inherent patterns of power, to expose and critique them, and to find approaches that will encourage equality.

Privilege Theory prompts us to ask self-reflective questions to educators. Because everyone belongs to some privileged category, everyone is implicated in this process (Ferber et al., 2009), and these questions could help shed light on all faculty members' self-awareness, attitudes, and behavior (inclusion/exclusion) toward other campus members.

In addition, Privilege Theory builds on CRT in its focus on the intersectionality of social identities. Recently, scholars have stressed the importance of a more intersectional approach to learning about diversity issues (Allen, 2004; Crenshaw, 1991; Ferber et al., 2009; Ore, 2006; Rothenberg, 2009; Segal & Martinez, 2007). Brewer and Pierce (2005) suggested that including a broad range of social group identities and their impact on the individual in diversity trainings can minimize bias and discrimination. The literature also suggests that diverse social group identities must be incorporated into our analyses and understanding of diversity, for when these multidimensional elements are absent, fundamental aspects of each individual's experience are excluded. Cultural inclusiveness must take all of our various social identities into account to be successful.

Social Identity Development

Social Identity Development theories provide insight into individuals' progression in terms of understanding how their social group memberships impact the ways they see themselves and others: both identity statuses that give them privilege and those that do not. These models generally depict a progression from lack of awareness of social constructs and inequalities to a fully developed multicultural activist consciousness. The latter includes awareness of the impact of one's own social identities on themselves and their behaviors toward others and, at the same time, embraces the social differences of others. Most Social Identity Development models are based on one social identity in particular: race. For example, Cross (1978) created a Black Identity Development model; Helms (1984, 1995) created a White Identity Development model; Sue (1981) developed an Asian Identity Development model; and Atkinson, Morten, and Sue (1983) created a multiracial model. In contrast, Hardiman and Jackson (1997) provided a multicultural model that is intersectional because it includes race, gender, sexual orientation, and so forth, and therefore, it is more useful for this research.

Hardiman and Jackson's Social Identity Development model consists of five stages: *naïve* (no social consciousness), *acceptance* (passive or active), *resistance* (passive or active), *redefinition*, and finally, *internalization*. Their *naïve* stage occurs during childhood, when awareness of one's social identities is still forming. They suggest that pushing against the boundaries of one's own identities is typically met with the policing of those boundaries by parents, guardians, teachers, and so on, thereby teaching an individual that there are differences between their own identities and those of others. The *acceptance* stage refers to the period when individuals passively or actively accept the stereotypes and myths that they have been taught about society. For example, most people are socialized in the United States to believe that we live in a meritocracy; that is, anyone who works hard enough can succeed. This belief ignores the systemic inequalities that make it so that those with privileged social group memberships (e.g., White people or males) are more likely to succeed when compared with others. Likewise, it ignores the fact that people without those privileged statuses are less likely to do well, regardless of how determined they are or how hard they work. Hardiman and Jackson's *acceptance* stage of their Social Identity Development model represents an adherence to societal ideologies such as meritocracy, equality, and individuality, among others.

The next phase in their model, the *resistance* stage, refers to individuals who resist the stereotypes and socially imposed norms of society that perpetuate social inequalities. People in this stage tend to be more aware of social inequalities and either passively or actively work to challenge these myths. For example, a teacher might be aware of the heterosexism embedded in the phrase "That's so gay" when his students use it to describe something negative (passive resistance) and choose to challenge his students to consider using a different phrase (active resistance). This stage is also marked by an attempt to recognize and challenge one's own internalized oppressive thoughts, beliefs, and attitudes, and the realization that it is possible to create social change by changing one's own behavior.

The fourth and fifth stages, *redefinition* and *internalization*, respectively, focus on identifying new ways of being in the world given the knowledge and understanding gained in stage three, and finally incorporating a more multicultural existence into one's everyday life. The progression from one stage to another can happen through the aging process as one has more multicultural experiences, though development can stall at any of the stages. Hardiman and Jackson made it clear that, as is the case with all Social Identity Development models, individuals do not necessarily go step-by-step from one stage to the next, but rather may progress forward and backward along the path as their development and understanding deepens. Even so, classroom cultural inclusiveness specifically revolves around stages two and three: *acceptance* and *resistance*, because educators, like most individuals, will likely be caught somewhere within or between these two stages. Samuels (2013b) has designated that space in between: the *discordance* stage, in which individuals demonstrate elements of both the *acceptance* and *resistance* stages. Many individuals can be so profoundly stuck in between those stages that their patterns of vacillation could even be considered a separate Social Identity Development stage of its own. For example, some individuals might acknowledge the existence of social privilege but at the same time adhere to colorblindness. It seems obvious that faculty members who are in the *resistance* stage or beyond will more likely be aware of social inequalities and their own efficacy to make a difference in this area, and thus will be more prepared to build cultural inclusiveness.

The importance of inclusiveness is clear. At a very basic level, inclusiveness means feeling a sense of belonging. Without that sense on a college campus, or in any educational setting, students and other institutional members are less likely to persist and achieve their goals. How prepared are faculty members for building cultural inclusiveness? This question will be considered in the next chapter.

CHAPTER 2

We're Not as Prepared as We Think We Are

> The greatest enemy of knowledge is not ignorance, it is the illusion of knowledge.
>
> —*Stephen Hawking*

I had the unique opportunity a few years back to attend a panel discussion at a conference called *Building Inclusiveness at CU* held at the University of Colorado at Colorado Springs (UCCS). The session was unique because the panel was comprised entirely of a group of UCCS students of color who came together to share their ideas about what they believed every faculty member should know about their own experiences as students of color. It gave me the chance to reflect on what I, and possibly other faculty members, staff, and administrators, might be missing or overlooking when it comes to the experiences of students of color on campus.

The first thing the students did when we entered the room was hand each of us a large adhesive label and a marker. They proceeded to make a list on the whiteboard of social identity categories and asked that we write on our labels our own statuses in each of those categories (White, female, lesbian, temporarily nondisabled, and so on). They then asked us to stick the labels to our chests to make our identities apparent to others, for as we know, some identities are visible while others are not. Next, they asked us to consider which of our identities provide benefits in our lives and which might keep us at a disadvantage at a systemic level. Most important, they asked us how those identities impact our lives, and especially, our teaching practices.

The panel of students explained the importance of faculty members' willingness and ability to recognize and verbalize to their students their privileged positions because they knew it impacted faculty members' teaching styles, curricula, and classroom environment. This was so critical to them, in fact, that one panelist stated, "If educators cannot locate themselves in terms of their privileged statuses, I know they'll never see me." In other words, if privilege is unstated and remains invisible, it is unlikely that a faculty member will acknowledge the unique experiences of students of color. This relatively short exercise taught us a significant amount about what it might be like to be part of a traditionally marginalized group (based on race, sexuality, socioeconomic status, disability, and so forth) and to sit among classmates who primarily represent the dominant culture, as is the case in so many educational institutions. As much as we might think we are prepared to build multicultural inclusiveness, both in and out of the classroom, are we really?

WHAT DOES IT MEAN TO BE PREPARED?

Several scholars have theorized about the concept of preparedness (Howard, 1999; Hurtado et al., 1998; Tatum, 2003), but little empirical research has been conducted to add to this literature or to their theories until now. That said, a body of literature does exist that measures teacher preparedness to teach "multicultural" students. Overwhelmingly, this refers to K–12 teachers and their preparedness to teach students of color specifically, as opposed to any other group of underrepresented students (e.g., lesbian/gay students, students with disabilities, students from lower socioeconomic classes). Nonetheless, a clear connection can be made between these skill sets (teaching students of color and teaching students who have been traditionally marginalized by other statuses). It can be argued that educators who are prepared to teach multicultural students are more likely to create and maintain a culturally inclusive environment. Thus, the research on multicultural preparedness provides a worthwhile starting point.

The changing demographics of the United States have created a substantive need to better prepare teachers for diverse classrooms (Ladson-Billings, 2005; Sobel, Iceman-Sands, & Basile, 2007). In fact, preparing teachers for more diverse classrooms is widely considered one of the greatest challenges facing educators in today's society (Futrell, Gomez, & Bedden, 2003; Hollins & Guzman, 2005; Sobel & Taylor, 2005). It would seem, therefore, that this would be a fertile topic in both K–12 and postsecondary arenas, but surprisingly, this is not the case.

Many more studies have been conducted on K–12 teachers in terms of measuring preparedness to teach multicultural students (Barry & Lechner, 1995; Futrell, 1999; Kea, Trent, & Davis, 2002; Kea & Utley, 1998; Ladson-Billings, 1999; McDermott, Rothenberg, & Gormley, 1999; McMackin & Bukowiecki, 1997; Sobel, Iceman-Sands, & Basile, 2007; Swartz & Bakari, 2005; Wiggins & Follo, 1999) than have been conducted on faculty of higher education (Grimm, 2000; Salcedo, 2003; Schuerholz-Lehr, 2007). And those studies that have been conducted at colleges or universities have not been national studies, but instead have been based on one specific campus. Nevertheless, all studies overwhelmingly produce the same results: Teachers do not feel prepared to teach multicultural students. Moreover, scholars suggest that the educational system has not sufficiently prepared educators to teach diverse populations (Ladson-Billings, 1999; Melnick & Zeichner, 1998; Zeichner & Hoeft, 1996).

At the turn of the 21st century, scholars began to delve into teacher education programs to try to figure out what was missing in teacher preparation for teaching diverse students. They found that the student teachers, much like their teacher education faculty, were overwhelmingly White, monolingual, and monocultural in terms of their background and experiences (Ducharme & Agne, 1989; Melnick & Zeichner, 1998). As a result, they had not had the opportunity to consider teaching in a multicultural setting and felt completely unprepared to do so (Ladson-Billings, 1999).

Further, there does not seem to be any particular organizational body that keeps comprehensive track of how the United States is doing in terms of building campus inclusiveness. The American Council on Education maintains statistical data on representativeness of campus members in colleges and universities (Diana Cordova, personal communication, February 24, 2009); however, representation is only one piece of an inclusiveness evaluation and, alone, is insufficient.

In addition, there are no current standards, national or otherwise, to assess diversity initiatives on campuses. Although there is a growing number of chief diversity officers (CDOs) on U.S. campuses, there are many campus employees who are tasked with diversity recruitment and/or retention who do not officially serve under the title of CDO (Williams & Wade-Golden, 2007). This makes it impossible to quantify this important institutionalized position. Furthermore, there are neither national standards for the difficult work these campus members do nor is there a way to compare one campus's successes with another's. If we want to be aware of the progress (or lack thereof) on campus inclusiveness, we clearly need better methods.

Many campuses include a diversity statement on their websites, demonstrating at least some level of commitment on the part of the administration to diversity and inclusiveness. Bluemel (2011) found that clearly communicating that diversity is a priority in the organization correlates with a more inclusive climate. The form this commitment takes, however, is not consistent among campuses. An informal web search of diversity statements of 4-year public institutions in Colorado, for example, demonstrated this inconsistency. Some campuses included a comprehensive diversity strategic plan, including recruitment and retention of all campus members, while others had no mention of diversity at all. Still others professed that they were making a commitment to diversity, but they either neglected to describe that commitment or focused only on a diverse student body and did not include the incorporation of diversity for all campus members (i.e., administration, staff, and faculty). Very few campuses described diversity initiatives specifically, and those that did rarely included a professional development program to teach faculty members how to better build campus diversity and inclusiveness.

This does not mean that faculty development around diversity and inclusiveness does not exist on campuses. First, though, there is no way to find out if it does; second, the lack of consistency across campuses makes these programs difficult to quantify; and third, the lack of information available makes it impossible to evaluate the quality of these programs. For example, are they intersectional? Are they successful? Do they incorporate the concept of privilege? Do they incorporate research into practice, using all available resources to make the program as successful as possible, or are they making it up as they go along? If these questions are not asked in a consistent way, how can we assess these programs? And if we do not ask these questions, are we really serving the needs of diverse campus populations?

Finally, assessment of diversity training is rare, if it exists at all (Chrobot-Mason & Quiñones, 2002; Hite & McDonald, 2006; Ivancevich & Gilbert, 2000; Roberson, Kulik, & Pepper, 2003). As a result, other than the few self-assessments conducted by training facilitators (Hite & McDonald, 2006; Morris, Romero, & Tan, 1996; Pendry, Driscoll, & Field, 2007), there are no standards to measure the success or failure of these trainings. Moreover, many diversity trainings are not developed using a theoretical framework, empirical evidence, or academic resources. Without assessment, they cannot be judged as to their usefulness (Hite & McDonald, 2006).

As previously mentioned, it is becoming more and more common to see campus climate surveys that describe how campus members (students, faculty, or staff) perceive the campus as a whole in terms of diversity issues. The Association of American Colleges and Universities offers a plethora of survey examples and suggestions on its website. These can serve as extreme ly effective tools for campus administrators who seek to understand the overall problems that might be occurring and need to be addressed. Most surveys ask respondents to rate how they feel the campus is doing in general in various areas such as discrimination, equality, and so forth. However, they typically do not include a mode of measuring the personal attitudes and behaviors of campus members.

It can be argued that faculty members are sometimes the strongest link between the university and the student. In fact, recent studies on the socialization process of students at a college or university (cultural awareness and inclusiveness, as well as social and political attitudes) have demonstrated that although it was commonly thought that peer groups have the strongest impact on students' socialization process, it is actually faculty who have a much stronger part to play than was thought (Hurtado, 1992; Milem, 1994).

Literature on this topic demonstrates a fundamental need for faculty members to be prepared to build cultural inclusiveness (Grant & Secada, 1990; Howard, 1999; Hurtado et al., 1998; Sadker & Sadker, 2009), but until now, there have been few empirical data available to assess the extent to which faculty consider themselves prepared, if they feel prepared at all. The research study described below tested the literature on preparedness to build cultural inclusiveness using a quantitative approach through the development of a survey instrument disseminated to a national random sample of faculty members.

PREPAREDNESS RESEARCH

The preparedness study I discuss in this book was based on a conceptual model that posited that preparedness to build cultural inclusiveness is comprised of five constructs. These are (1) perceptions of social inequalities/attitudes about diversity, (2) consideration of social group memberships, (3) self-reflection on biases and behaviors, (4) intention/self-efficacy to build inclusiveness, and (5) behavioral outcomes. The model is depicted in Figure 2.1.

Perceptions of Social Inequalities/Attitudes About Diversity

Zeichner (1993) theorized that one of the many traditions of teacher education is a social reconstructionist approach. That is, education and teacher training serve as one aspect of social reform that leads society toward social justice and equity. This tradition asks prospective teachers to consider social inequalities that exist in society and what their own contribution might be toward social change (Ladson-Billings, 1999). This idea leads to the formation of the first subconstruct in the survey instrument (see Appendix A): faculty members' perceptions of social inequalities and attitudes about diversity.

Perceptions of Social Inequalities. Throughout history, some have argued that the United States is the *land of equal opportunity*—a meritocracy in which everyone can reach their goals and realize their aspirations if they simply work hard and take advantage of the opportunities that surround them. According to this approach, success depends solely upon personal ambition coupled with talent and/or intellectual ability; conversely, failure

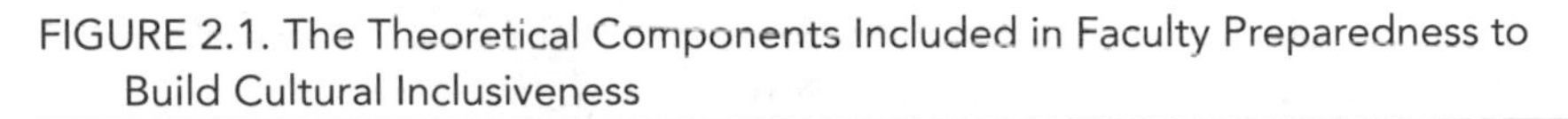

FIGURE 2.1. The Theoretical Components Included in Faculty Preparedness to Build Cultural Inclusiveness

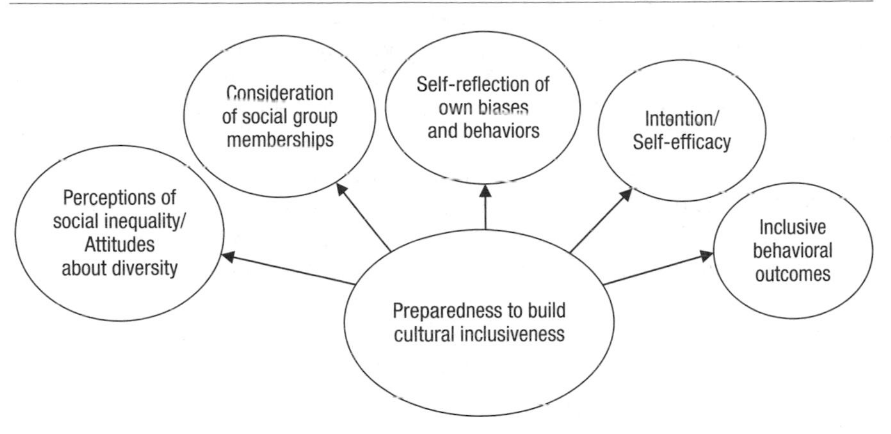

is the result of the *natural* or innate differences among us. The American dream is the desire to live in a society in which *everyone* has the opportunity to be successful and reach their life potential. In reality, however, the American dream has and continues to be unattainable for many of our nation's citizens (Bonilla-Silva, 2009; Ferber et al., 2009; Gallagher, 2009; Johnson, 2006; Kozol, 2005).

Today, we live in a highly stratified society—a society in which people are divided and ranked hierarchically according to various categories such as race, ethnicity, gender, social class, disability, and sexuality, and these rankings lead to inequality. For example, a tremendous gap exists between the very wealthy and the very poor in our society, women still earn less money than men for working at the same jobs, and people of color are disproportionately less educated and underpaid compared with White people. Some might argue that the reason for these discrepancies lies in the inherent differences that exist among us. For many, this answer provides a simple or convenient explanation for the inequality that exists today between men and women and between people of color and Whites, and, moreover, rationalizes and justifies the status quo (Bonilla-Silva, 2009; Ferber et al., 2009; Gallagher, 2009; Johnson, 2006; Kozol, 2005).

In actuality, inequality is the result of hundreds of years of social, political, and economic oppression and privilege that many people do not take into account or of which they are not even aware (see Sen, 1990; Sobel, 2002; and Stronks, 1997 for alternate discussions). To better appreciate the paths that faculty members might take in developing knowledge and understanding of social inequalities and their impact on individuals, it is useful to consider the Social Identity Development model presented in Chapter 1.

Once again, Hardiman and Jackson (1997) found that most people fall in either their *acceptance* stage or *resistance* stage, or somewhere in between. To reiterate, the *acceptance* stage describes an individual who lacks any awareness of social constructs and inequalities, has learned societal ideologies such as equality and individuality, and accepts them, unchallenged. The *resistance* stage describes those who have become aware through education or experience that societal ideologies are often myths and do not represent reality. They realize that social inequalities exist based on one's social group memberships. They begin to challenge those myths and realize their own roles both in perpetuating the myths and challenging them. Acknowledging social inequalities is a critical step in the process of building cultural inclusiveness because doing so emphasizes the systemic nature of inequalities and the impact that society has on the individual's experiences. Thus, it is more likely that a faculty member in the *resistance* stage will be better prepared to build cultural inclusiveness than one who is in the *acceptance* stage.

Attitudes About Diversity. Faculty members' attitudes about diversity are often rooted in their perceptions of inequality. If faculty members acknowledge that social inequalities exist in society as a consequence of larger systemic forces, then they are likely to have different attitudes about diversity than they would if they failed to acknowledge this.

Mezirow (1994) used the term *meaning scheme* to describe individuals' frame of reference, their beliefs, attitudes, and judgments that provide the basis of a person's worldview, which are used to interpret their surroundings. In order to predict people's intentions or behavior, it is helpful to understand their worldviews. Mezirow claimed that our attitudes about those who are members of different social groups from our own are often based on assumptions learned through "cultural assimilation in childhood" (p. 223). This notion is similar to Hardiman and Jackson's *acceptance* stage in their Social Identity Development model. Allport (1979) also concluded that prejudices are created in early childhood. This does not mean that attitudes cannot change over time; on the contrary, research shows that they can (Chang, 2002; J. H. Katz, 1977; Milner, Flowers, Moore, Moore, & Flowers, 2003).

It is also important to acknowledge the influence that our status has on our own attitudes and behavior. In other words, our social group statuses directly impact our experience in the world. As was stated in Chapter 1, the ways in which we are privileged affects our life chances, the impressions we make on others, and our own sense of identity (Ferber et al., 2009). It is imperative, therefore, to acknowledge the statuses that privilege us (masculinity, Whiteness, heterosexuality, and so on) to help us become aware of the ways we may be including some people and excluding others (D. R. Samuels, 2009a).

In addition, acknowledging privilege exposes the social hierarchy rather than keeping it invisible. In general, because privilege is often omitted from the discussion, it is not considered in the equation of inequality. As Johnson (2006) suggests, however:

> A common form of blindness to privilege is that women and people of color are often described as being treated unequally, but men and whites are not. This, however, is logically impossible. *Unequal* simply means "not equal," which describes both those who receive less than their fair share *and* those who receive more. (p. 120)

Privilege Theory challenges individuals to make the invisible visible. The preparedness study outlined below highlights this notion by asking faculty members to consider the ways in which some of their own social statuses carry privilege and might contribute, even unintentionally, to the exclusion of others.

Allen (2004) noted that recognizing our own privilege can be difficult but is necessary if we hope to learn to build inclusiveness. She suggested that we examine our own attitudes and thoughts and "look for evidence of dominant belief systems" (p. 191). Ignoring one's privileged status, Jensen (2009) argues, is the ultimate privilege—a privilege that those with visible nondominant statuses do not enjoy. Incorporating Privilege Theory into the research project is a crucial component of measuring preparedness to build cultural inclusiveness.

Attitude-Behavior Relation Theory. Further, attitude-behavior relation theory adds to these other ideas by stating that if a person's attitude is altered through an experience or learning process, then it is extremely likely that the person's actions will also change. Two elements make it more likely that attitudes will translate into action: The attitudes in question must be specific as opposed to general, and the attitudes must relate directly to the action. If both of these criteria are met, then altered behavior can be predictable based on one's attitudes (Ajzen & Fishbein, 1977; Davidson & Jaccard, 1979). This important concept has implications not only if we want to justify querying faculty members on their attitudes around inclusiveness, but also for predicting their behavior.

In addition, this theory has implications for the use of the survey instrument as a pre- and postassessment of faculty diversity initiatives. The research of Ajzen and Fishbein (1977) and Davidson and Jaccard (1979) suggested that it might be possible to affect attitudes and behavior as long as specific, corresponding behaviors are cited and encouraged during a diversity training session and participants agree that they might consider changing their behavior. Although some scholars agree that changing racist behavior, specifically, is difficult (Hersey & Blanchard, 1969; Zimbardo & Ebbesen, 1970), J. H. Katz (1977) argued that attitude change can occur through the process of receiving and incorporating new knowledge. Moreover, Mezirow (1994) explained the process of transformative learning as "the social process of construing and appropriating a new or revised interpretation of the meaning of one's experience as a guide to action" (pp. 222–223).

According to these ideas, it is likely that altered behavior can, in fact, occur as a result of diversity training. Evaluating the degree to which the attitudes of participants have been transformed from before to after training can provide insight into possible changes in behavior and can serve as an assessment of the effectiveness of the training. Overall, measuring attitudes provides insight into an individual's experiences and worldview, and someone's readiness to build cultural inclusiveness.

Consideration of Social Group Memberships

Another aspect of preparedness to build cultural inclusiveness revolves around faculty members' consideration of the way social group memberships influence their interactions with others. First, it is important to acknowledge how our perceptions, experiences, and attitudes contribute to how we treat others who have different social group memberships from our own. Over the past several decades, psychologists have made connections between internalized impressions about race and ethnicity, and discrimination and racism (Dovidio & Gaertner, 1997; Jones, 1997; P. A. Katz, 1983). These connections demonstrate that what we believe to be true, we may be more likely to act on. As a result, it is critical to consider faculty members' attitudes about others' social group memberships as a critical component of understanding how they may act toward other campus members.

One way to transform our attitudes is by viewing the world through another person's perspective (perspective taking), which creates awareness of other people's situations (Pendry, Driscoll, & Field, 2007); this is also known as *critical awareness* (Kirkham, Van Hofwegen, & Harwood, 2005). Awareness of social inequalities can effectively change a person's attitude about certain social group memberships. For example, research shows that when we are exposed to another individual's lived experiences (such as those of an elderly person), we become less likely to rely on stereotypic ideas about that person's social group (Galinsky & Moskowitz, 2000). In fact, psychological research suggests that when the differences between individuals are emphasized, prejudicial attitudes can increase (Bodenhausen

& Macrae, 1994; Paluck, 2006). Perspective taking, on the other hand, allows individuals to find similarities between themselves and others, more so than they might expect (Dovidio, Gaertner, Stewart, Esses, & ten Vergert, 2004). This is apparent in the research of Wentling, Schilt, Windsor, and Lucal (2008). They found that assessing one's preconceived notions about transgender individuals and learning about other people through perspective taking promotes more inclusive teaching practices.

Self-Reflection of Biases and Behaviors

Consideration of social statuses and their impact on behavior, however, is not enough to assess a faculty member's preparedness to build cultural inclusiveness. What is needed in addition is an element of personal responsibility: an acknowledgment of biased behavior and an intention to change it (Pendry, Driscoll, & Field, 2007). Many scholars agree that multicultural teacher preparation must include an exploration into a teacher's own experiences (Banks, 1995; Boyle-Baise & Sleeter, 1996; R. J. Martin, 1991). It is important for faculty members to reflect on their assumptions, attitudes, values, and experiences (Cochran-Smith, 1995a; Schoorman, 2002; Tan, Morris, & Romero, 1996; Wasonga, 2005). As Allen (2004) suggests, we must "begin within" (p. 291). Teachers must make the connection between our own identities and histories and the way our experiences affect both our current beliefs and our interactions with others.

This is not an easy process. Mezirow (1994) argues that the way we make sense of the world can be transformed through reflection. The process of reflection begins with an experience or information that triggers what he refers to as a "disorienting dilemma" (p. 224). This dilemma prompts us to examine ourselves and our long-held assumptions about the world. Kirkham et al. (2005) suggested that "disorienting experiences set in motion critical reflection that involve[s] adapting conceptual structures previously relied upon for meaning making" (p. 8). Disorienting dilemmas also push us to question whether or not those assumptions are grounded in reality and to consider the consequences of maintaining our long-held beliefs. Therefore, asking faculty members to reflect on the ways they treat others is a critical component of their preparedness to build cultural inclusiveness. If they do not engage in self-reflection, it is possible that they might be less willing or able to create deep, long-lasting change (Samuels & Samuels, 2003).

Intention/Self-Efficacy

Intention can be considered a bridge between one's attitudes and one's actions. Self-efficacy is the belief that we can act.

Intention. An intention to act is a precursor to specifically decided-upon behavior. Bandura (2001) stated:

> An intention is a representation of a future course of action to be performed. It is not simply an expectation or prediction of future actions but a proactive commitment to bringing them about. Intentions and actions are different aspects of a functional relation separated in time. (p. 6)

Bandura suggests that our intention or, in other words, our self-directedness, motivates and shapes our behavior. This is accomplished through a process of self-monitoring our thoughts and behaviors, keeping in mind our own values, while at the same time considering the sociocultural context in which we exist.

Fiske (1989) states that intent is comprised of three elements: (1) having a choice and the ability to decide between the alternatives, (2) choosing the more difficult path, and (3) consciously choosing to pay specific attention to some aspects of a situation and not others. Fiske uses the example of stereotyping to demonstrate this idea. The first element includes the assumption that person A knows that they have the ability to stereotype person B; the second element incorporates the assumption that person A chooses *not* to stereotype; and the third element assumes that person A chooses to focus on person B as an individual rather than as a member of a stereotypic group. In the same vein as Powell's (2012) concept of "priming," Lewin (1951) proposed that intent prepares a person for a different behavioral outcome by changing the way in which we perceive a situation. Exploring our intentions provides insight into our willingness to engage in inclusive behavior.

Intention by itself, however, is not an effective measurement of preparedness to build cultural inclusiveness either, because, as Gay (2000) pointed out, "Intention without action is insufficient" (p. 13). A faculty member may possess both positive attitudes about diversity and be self-reflective, but still may not feel prepared to act. They may instead feel overwhelmed by the task at hand and perhaps even think that small actions cannot make a difference in society or in the world. Without the intention, motivation, and understanding that small changes can, in fact, impact others—especially students—a faculty member would not be prepared to build inclusiveness.

Johnson (2006) described this situation as "Gandhi's Paradox and the Myth of No Effect" (p. 131). He suggests that if individuals believe they have to take on racism, for example, and eradicate it by themselves, and that that is the only way they can make a difference, then any efforts on their part are perceived to be too small to matter: That is, the problem is just too big. Regardless, Johnson insists that it is important to act. He states, "Gandhi once said that nothing we do as individuals matters but that it's vitally important to do it anyway" (p. 132). It goes along with the popular allegory of the starfish (which has been adapted from Eiseley, 1969). On a hot, sunny day, a man slowly walks down a beach that is completely covered with starfish that had been washed ashore in the aftermath of a great rain. The man stoops down and gently picks up one starfish at a time, hurling each one back into the cool water to be revived. When asked what the point was, why such a seemingly futile exercise matters, his response was, "Well, it mattered to *that* starfish." The enormity of the problem cannot stop us from our intention to create social change.

Self-Efficacy. Still, we need to believe we have the ability to make a difference. Bandura (1986), the leading theorist on self-efficacy, defined it as:

> people's judgments of their capabilities to organize and execute courses of action required to attain designated types of performances. It is concerned not with the skills one has but with judgments of what one can do with whatever skills one possesses. (p. 391)

Bandura (2001) claims that without both a belief in our ability to affect positive change and confidence that our actions can guard against unfavorable outcomes, we would have no motivation to take action or to persist when problems arise. He suggests that individuals need personal agency to act. He defined personal agency as "the power to originate actions for given purposes" (p. 6). Making use of Social Cognitive Theory, he describes three kinds of agency: (1) direct personal agency, (2) proxy agency (giving someone else the power to make choices for you), and (3) collective agency (working together with others to achieve consensus). Direct personal agency informs the current preparedness study in that "it is partly on the basis of efficacy beliefs that people choose what challenges to undertake . . . [and] how much effort to expend in the endeavor" (p. 10). Self-efficacy, then, is another critical aspect of preparedness in that the likelihood that people will act depends greatly on their belief that they can, in fact, bring about change.

Page and Czuba (1999) connected Bandura's (1986) Self-Efficacy Theory with the concept of *empowerment*. They define empowerment as "a process that fosters power (that is, the capacity to implement) in people, for use in their own lives, their communities, and in their society by acting on issues that they define as important" (para. 11). Here, Page and Czuba add the element of power to the concept of self-efficacy. In other words, empowerment can be considered the ability and confidence to influence others or outcomes. This is slightly different from self-efficacy in that the focus is on the external outcome as opposed to the internal willingness and ability to act.

Though the current preparedness study that I conducted centers on self-efficacy and internal perceptions of the motivation to act, empowerment is worth considering in terms of Page and Czuba's definition. Their explanation of empowerment mirrors Bandura's suggestion to consider self-efficacy in a sociocultural context, and includes the impact of society on what the individual defines as important. The definition suggests that people might only act on issues that they consider important. As a result, the survey instrument in the current research (see Appendix A) specifically asked whether or not faculty members consider the issue of campus inclusiveness important. If they do not agree that it is important, then they are not likely to be prepared to work toward building it. In the context of the current research study, intention, self-efficacy, and the premium they place on diversity and inclusiveness are all vital to a faculty member's preparedness for building cultural inclusiveness.

Behavioral Outcomes

Many scholars in the fields of psychology, health, sociology, and education argue that attitudes, self-reflection, and motivation to change are contributors to action, but K. M. Brown (2004) maintained that reflection and understanding are only worthwhile if they do, in fact, lead to social action. Kirkham et al. (2005) suggested that critical awareness leads to *critical engagement* (discordance and self-scrutiny) and a resulting (re)dedication to *social change* (transformation). These ideas are based in part on Paulo Freire's (1993) theory of conscientization. This theory revolves around the idea that society is made up of systems of inequality that must be actively challenged by individuals. These notions pave the way for personal empowerment: the notion that individuals can take action and work to change systemic oppression. Freire combined theory and practice to educate and motivate. Within this praxis, individuals can engage in political action when they collaborate with others to gain a "critical consciousness" and begin to understand the ways in which oppression operates; they then become empowered to act.

Kirkham et al. (2005) posited that this transformation can be much more successful when an individual is surrounded by or immersed in a supportive environment. Schugurensky (2002) agreed and offered three elements that can contribute to transformation: (1) an accommodating social climate, (2) a collective commitment toward a similar goal, and (3) a connection to community. These elements are corroborated by campus inclusiveness scholars who suggest that conditions on a campus must be receptive and conducive to inclusiveness in order to be successful (Hurtado et al., 1998).

A supportive community is important to building inclusiveness and is first and foremost the responsibility of the campus administration, but educators also have a responsibility to their students to teach inclusively. Although some teachers say they are open to the idea of inclusive behavior, Martin and Williams-Dixon (1994) found that many preservice teachers' actions were not actually inclusive. In their study, they found that respondents said they welcome diversity, yet also said they were accepting of racist jokes, thought any statements about race made in the classroom should be ignored, and believed that students of color tended to get defensive when racial statements were made. In another study, Terrill and Mark (2000) found that although 75% of those preservice teachers surveyed said they hoped to be placed in a school that required teachers to learn Spanish to better communicate with Hispanic students, most teachers asked to be placed in a White suburban school. These are just a few examples of behavioral outcomes that are rooted in prejudice. If educators are not aware of how their own behavior can create an inclusive or an exclusive environment, it is not likely that they will work toward inclusiveness.

Many educators, on the other hand, may have positive attitudes about diversity and want to make a difference, but simply do not know how to do so. An entire body of literature has been dedicated to Culturally Responsive Teaching. Gay (2000) defined Culturally Responsive Teaching as "using the cultural knowledge, prior experience, frames of references, and performance styles of ethnically diverse students to make learning encounters more relevant to and effective for them. It teaches to and through the strengths of these students" (p. 29). She added that students' experience of Culturally Responsive Teaching is "validating and affirming" (p. 29). Neal, Webb-Johnson, and McCray (2003) add that Culturally Responsive Teaching provides a mutually beneficial setting for teachers and learners. Students view teachers who use Culturally Responsive Teaching in their classrooms as role models, and the teachers consider their students "culturally strong, cooperative, academically able, and integral members of the classroom" (p. 30). Culturally Responsive Teaching is one method of incorporating inclusive behaviors into the classroom and informs the survey instrument discussed below in terms of the kinds of diversity it includes (racial, learning styles, engagement styles, and so on).

Other scholars have focused on best practices for teaching inclusively. Chickering and Gamson (1999), for example, focus on active learning strategies for educators and how to include diverse ways of learning into the curriculum. Salisbury and Goodman (2009) present a list of educational good practices that include, among other ideas, engaging students in the process of making connections to historical, political, and social issues so that they see the systemic impact of the material and are able to apply what they are learning. Many strategies, articles, and reports were reviewed for the study outlined below to consider best practices for building inclusiveness in the classroom. In order to assess a faculty member's preparedness in terms of behavioral outcomes and according to the aforementioned literature in psychology, it was necessary to ask specific questions about behavior.

PREPAREDNESS STUDY

I found no scales that specifically measured faculty preparedness to build cultural inclusiveness, thus it became incumbent upon me to create and test my own. There are many campus climate surveys that tend to measure the cultural environment on a campus, and how the institution is faring in terms of diversity, but they do not tend to delve into the actual attitudes and intentions of faculty members. The survey instrument I created (see Appendix A) was informed by the literature as well as existing scales, and attempted to measure the proposed latent construct of faculty *preparedness* to build cultural inclusiveness. The survey included 27 items that represented each of the five components of preparedness, all measured on a 7-point Likert-type scale, and concluded with demographic questions.

This instrument was tested on a national random sample of 637 faculty members to determine how prepared they are to build cultural inclusiveness. Unlike other campus climate surveys, this instrument focuses on faculty members' attitudes, consideration of social group memberships, self-awareness of biases, intention, and behavioral outcomes (which, as previously noted, were the five factors in the structural model). In addition, unlike other surveys, this one is intersectional, covering issues of gender, race, sexual orientation, and disability, among others.

Of the 637 faculty members who responded to the survey, 79% identified as White and 12.4% identified as people of color. Because the national average for faculty is approximately 80% White, this sample was accurately representative of White faculty; faculty of color, however, were slightly underrepresented in this sample, as the national average is approximately 17% (U.S. Department of Education, 2009). There were 55 respondents (8.6%) who chose not to identify their race.

Females comprised 54% of respondents, which is higher than the national average of female faculty (42%). Males made up 45.5% of respondents, which is lower than the national average of male faculty (58%) (U.S. Department of Education, 2007), and one faculty member identified as transgender. Just over 88% of respondents identified themselves as heterosexual; 7% identified as lesbian, gay, bisexual, or queer/questioning; and 4.3% chose not to respond. The 637 faculty members ranged in age from

23 to 83, and came from every kind of institution, including public, private, and military academies; both 2-year and 4-year institutions; and from all academic fields.

To analyze the data, the sample was randomly split into two groups. Exploratory factor analysis (EFA) was conducted. Consistent with the theoretical framework, five factors emerged. Structural Equation Modeling (SEM) confirmed the EFA findings and showed that a revised version of the structural equation model produced a good fit to the data. The survey instrument demonstrated strong internal consistency (all alphas above .85). (Methodology for this research is included in Appendix A.)

As previously mentioned, preparedness has rarely been studied quantitatively, and to my knowledge, no study has been conducted using a national sample. As mentioned in Chapter 1, Howard's book (1999) *We Can't Teach What We Don't Know* theorizes a lack of preparedness among educators to teach in a growing multicultural society. The current study that forms the basis for this book suggests that this theory can be quantified and, further, that the extent to which a faculty member is prepared can be measured.

Contrary to the literature in the field, in this survey, on average, faculty members had relatively high scores on each of the five sublatent constructs of preparedness, demonstrating that they perceive themselves to be prepared to build cultural inclusiveness. If, on average, faculty members in this national study considered themselves prepared to build cultural inclusiveness, then how do we reconcile these findings with the theoretical framework of the research and the few studies that have been conducted in this area (described in Chapter 1) that have suggested faculty members are not, in fact, prepared? One hypothesis is that perhaps, based on the national sample and the robust design of the current research, faculty members are, in fact, more prepared to build cultural inclusiveness than has been previously thought. It is possible that based on the recent increase in focus on diversity and inclusiveness, faculty members are beginning to acknowledge the role they can play in building inclusiveness and are working toward this end.

Another hypothesis is that perhaps the discrepancy is in faculty members' beliefs about their own preparedness. In other words, it is possible that in the present study, faculty members demonstrated more confidence in their preparedness to build cultural inclusiveness than was actually the case. In other words, it is worth considering the possibility that faculty members may have overestimated their responses on the factors of preparedness. Research demonstrates that this could be a reasonable prospect. Social Desirability Theory, for example, describes the tendency of test-takers to present themselves in a positive light based on the socially constructed norms or standards of their culture or society (Crowne & Marlowe, 1964; Ganster, Hennessey, & Luthans, 1983; Humm & Humm, 1944; Nunnally, 1978). Based on the current cultural expectation to be respectful and accepting of diversity, Social Desirability Theory presents a plausible explanation for respondents' possible overestimation of their responses.

Looking at it another way, scholars have found that prejudice emerges from a sociocultural context—specifically, from stereotypes that are taught and often internalized, that are believed, and that can be acted upon. At the same time, social pressures can motivate individuals to control their feelings of prejudice because it is socially undesirable to be considered prejudiced. In their empirical research, Dunton and Fazio (1997) and Devine (1989) found that prejudiced individuals can choose to control their prejudice either because they do not want to be perceived by others as prejudiced, or because they do not want to perceive themselves as such. Either way, this motivation to control prejudice can have a strong effect on an individual's self-perception, and may help explain why respondents' scores were so high on each factor. I do not mean to assume that faculty members are necessarily prejudiced, but rather that they may perceive themselves as less prejudiced than they happen to be.

Perceptions of Social Inequalities/Attitudes About Diversity

On average, faculty members "somewhat agreed" that social inequalities exist, and that they are personally accepting of diversity. The responses to this factor contained the largest variability of any of the five factors of preparedness. This suggests that some respondents disagree that social inequalities exist, while others agree. The fact that not every respondent is in agreement on this issue might challenge the theoretical notion that inequalities exist for many members of traditionally oppressed groups. Contrarily, it might substantiate the literature in terms of a lack of knowledge as to the reality of social inequalities (Gallagher, 2009).

Further, considering the results in light of Social Identity Development theory, it is likely that many of the respondents could be situated in Hardiman and Jackson's (1997) *acceptance* stage. Once again, people in this stage of development tend to adhere to societal ideologies such as meritocracy, equality, and individuality, and tend to be either unaware or ignorant of the realities of unequal social systems and their consequences. Given that the responses to this factor produced, on average, a "somewhat agree" rather than a "somewhat disagree," it is likely that faculty members are more likely unaware or unsure of those inequalities as opposed to vehemently disagreeing that they exist.

Finally, it could also be argued that if many faculty members are unsure or unaware that social inequalities exist, it is likely that they do not see their own social statuses as holding privilege, making it less likely they are creating an inclusive environment for their students (Allen, 2004).

Consideration of Social Group Memberships

On average, faculty members "agree" or "strongly agree" that they are comfortable interacting with people on campus who are different from them in terms of social group memberships. This relatively high mean (the highest of all five factors) is, on the surface, a positive finding in terms of preparedness to build cultural inclusiveness. That is, as indicated by Privilege Theory and substantiated by the preparedness structural model in the study that is the basis for this book, a respondent's comfort level in interacting with others who have different social group memberships from their own is associated with preparedness for building cultural inclusiveness. The findings show that faculty members have a high comfort level, on average, and so they are, in fact, prepared in this way.

An alternative explanation for this relatively high mean, however, might be that colorblindness (or identity-blindness) was the goal for some faculty members, that perhaps they saw themselves as trying to ignore differences and made the assumption that they treat everyone "the same" (Bonilla-Silva, 2009). Consequently, they may have considered themselves comfortable with others who are different from them. As mentioned in the literature and in Chapter 1, colorblindness is a form of racism because it discounts the experiences of those in nondominant groups. Colorblindness, therefore, could certainly affect faculty members' preparedness to build cultural inclusiveness.

Self-Reflection of Biases and Behaviors

On average, faculty members "agree" that they consciously treat diverse campus members with both respect and acceptance. This is a positive step toward preparedness to build inclusiveness because it demonstrates faculty members' belief and confidence in how they treat people who are members of different social groups from their own. On the other hand, it is also important to consider the literature on the concept of microaggressions discussed in Chapter 1. It is possible that faculty members may think they are treating diverse campus members with respect and may not realize that they may unknowingly and unintentionally be perpetuating covert forms of oppression.

Intention/Self-Efficacy

On average, faculty members "agreed" that it is their responsibility to build campus inclusiveness, that they can have an impact on campus inclusiveness, and that they intend to do so. This is another positive finding in terms of faculty preparedness to build cultural inclusiveness. As Bandura (2001) suggests in Self-Efficacy Theory, intent is a precursor to action. The theory suggests that faculty members who are aware that they can influence campus inclusiveness, and are empowered to act, may be more likely to do so.

Respondents were more likely to acknowledge that building campus inclusiveness is their responsibility than to assert that they have the skills to build inclusiveness. This is an important finding for policy administrators in that it is an acknowledgment that there is a recognition of accountability—in other words, there is a ready and willing faculty, who may not have the skills needed to build inclusiveness.

The connection between intent and behavior, as outlined in the literature (Bandura, 2001; Fiske, 1989; Gay, 2000; Lewin, 1951; Page & Czuba, 1999), was affirmed in the current study for this book. A regression analysis demonstrated that a one-unit increase in intention/self-efficacy significantly predicted a .6-unit increase in inclusive behavior ($p < .001$). In other words, the more faculty members perceive that they can make a difference in building campus inclusiveness, and the more they are empowered to do so, the more likely they are to take action.

Behavioral Outcomes

On average, faculty members "somewhat agree" that they engage in culturally inclusive behaviors. If, on average, faculty members are taking action to build inclusiveness, then perhaps this shows that they are, in fact, more prepared to build cultural inclusiveness than was theorized in the literature. Yet, faculty members were more likely to agree that they *intend* to build inclusiveness than they are to act. There exists, then, a substantial disconnect for them. This result corroborates Martin and William-Dixon's (1994) previously mentioned finding that although teachers agreed that they were open to the idea of inclusive behavior, their actions were not inclusive.

It is likely, then, that based on the high scores on intention and the relatively low scores on behavior, on average, faculty members would like to be more inclusive, but simply do not have the knowledge or skills to do so. This result affirmed the literature both on Culturally Responsive Teaching and on Chickering and Gamson's (1999) best practices for teaching inclusively, which stated that in order to build campus inclusiveness, campuses must educate faculty on how to do so.

Meaningful Education on Diversity and Inclusiveness

Multicultural education is a substantial need on campuses, evidenced by respondents' testimony that, on average, they were not explicitly educated on diversity and inclusiveness, nor did their current institutions provide "meaningful education" on these topics. Moreover, those few who claimed that their institution did provide "meaningful education" were more likely to hold *negative* (or exclusionary) attitudes about diversity.

This finding is intriguing, but not surprising. It supports a recent study conducted by the Palm Center at University of California Santa Barbara, which surveyed 545 U.S. service members who had served in Iraq and Afghanistan since 2001. The study found that military personnel who received antigay harassment training were *less* supportive of the open service of gay and lesbian service members, as compared with those who did not receive such training (Moradi & Miller, 2009). One explanation Moradi and Miller suggest for this finding is the possibility that, contrary to the goals of the training, the content may, in fact, have reified the notion that lesbian and gay soliders serving openly might be harmful to military cohesion, and could provoke the harassment of these soldiers.

On the other hand, another study that might shed light on this finding investigates not the content of training, but the attitudes and behaviors of the trainer. Behavioral integrity is a perceived pattern of word-deed alignment (Simons, 2002) and demands consideration of how supervisors' (or trainers', in this context) attitudes and behaviors are perceived by subordinates (trainees) during training. In other words, behavioral integrity proposes inquiry into the extent to which trainers are exhibiting the desired behavior that the training is presumed to espouse. Put another way, if diversity trainees perceive that the trainers are not acting in accordance with what they espouse, then trainees are more likely to reject the content that is being taught, and their attitudes and behavior will demonstrate this resistance.

It is possible that either of these studies can serve to illuminate the findings of the current research examined in this book in that perhaps the diversity and inclusiveness trainings provided on campuses are not effective in producing the outcomes they hope to generate. Although the behavioral outcomes of faculty members may not be the only reason a campus might provide diversity and inclusiveness training, it is interesting to note that those faculty members whose campuses do provide "meaningful" diversity and inclusiveness education were no more or less likely to behave inclusively than those whose campuses did not provide such education. One explanation for this might be based on whether the "meaningful" education was mandatory or voluntary. Mandatory training could negatively affect the extent to which a faculty member engages in the training, and can impact behavioral outcomes (Paluck, 2006; van Dick et al., 2004). Lastly, the fact that only 35% of respondents agreed or strongly agreed that their current institution provided meaningful education on diversity and inclusiveness might imply a lack of commitment by colleges and universities to these issues.

It should be noted that those faculty members who stated that diversity and inclusiveness were an explicit part of their *graduate* education were more likely to behave inclusively. It seems there is a difference between receiving this education *before* teaching as opposed to receiving it as part of faculty development. It is possible that this difference might be attributed to the time involved in the education. In other words, perhaps in a graduate school context, diversity and inclusiveness training might consist of a full-semester course or even be incorporated in an entire graduate program. On the contrary, many faculty diversity-training initiatives consist of a few hours of training. The difference in behavior between these two groups could be attributed to the difference in the time spent learning about these issues. Once again, however, only 26% of respondents agreed or strongly agreed that they received this graduate training at all.

Although the current preparedness study discussed in this book surveyed college faculty, the results may be generalizable to K–12 educators as well, based on the fact that K–12 teachers have the same social context and subsequent biases as well as similar training before they teach. The findings on meaningful diversity and inclusiveness training were perhaps among the most important to this research in terms of asking: How can we expect educators to be successful at building inclusiveness if they have not had effective instruction to do so? Furthermore, what does effective instruction look like?

CHAPTER 3

Becoming Prepared

Feminist education—the feminist classroom—is and should be a place where there is a sense of struggle, where there is visible acknowledgment of the union of theory and practice, where we work together as teachers and students to overcome the estrangement and alienation that have become so much the norm in the contemporary university.

—*bell hooks*

Back in 2008, my colleague Christina Jiménez and I were asked by the associate vice chancellor for diversity and inclusiveness on our campus to create curriculum for a campus-wide diversity and inclusiveness workshop. Campus-wide meant that the workshops would be offered to faculty, staff, administrators, and student leaders. Because we had previously worked together developing a course called Introduction to Race and Gender for the Women's and Ethnic Studies program, we felt this was a challenging task, but achievable. We worked diligently for months deciding which aspects of diversity and inclusiveness we could fit into a 3-hour workshop. We called the training the "BIG Idea" Workshop; *BIG* stood for "Building Inclusiveness Group." Our objectives were to bring awareness, knowledge, and an opportunity for skill building to our campus. We made sure to highlight the concepts of oppression and privilege, and to make the workshop as intersectional as possible by bringing in information about inequities based on race, gender, social class, age, disability, sexual orientation, and other identities.

We then facilitated a pilot workshop with faculty who were on board with these concepts and whom we knew would offer us meaningful insight and suggestions, which they did. Over the course of the next few years, the workshops were offered to hundreds, if not thousands, of campus members. Our evaluations were generally excellent, with occasional complaints. I consider the endeavor successful overall, but my takeaways from the experience might be useful.

The workshops were positive in that they brought people from around campus together to engage in conversations around social identities, stereotypes, and inclusive behavior. The workshops also initiated a campus-wide discussion of the notion of privilege, including a speaker series on the topic, sponsored by the campus library. Further, the program was an important step for our campus to take in terms of making an obvious commitment in dedicating resources to make the campus inclusive.

What I learned over time, after cofacilitating the workshops countless times for various groups of campus members, was that these issues can be extremely challenging to people, especially if the concepts are new to them. Based on a mixed-methods study I conducted in order to gauge how we could improve the program, I learned that it was important to provide information, but not to lecture. The workshop curriculum included a folder of handouts and resources that provided so much information that it sometimes felt overwhelming to participants. Although the workshops were interactive, participants' evaluations suggested having less content (they could look at the resources later) and more hands-on activities. Without exception, participants agreed the 3-hour time period was not long enough to cover the ambitious objectives of the workshop.

Although the curriculum was designed to minimize resistance to issues of inequality and privilege, it was clear that facilitators had to be skilled and experienced in handling resistance, and that cofacilitation (preferably cofacilitators who had visibly different social identities—a woman and a man, a person of color and a White person, and so on) works well, so that if one facilitator is struggling with a resistant participant, the other facilitator can step in and explain things with a slightly different tone and style. Overall, this diversity and inclusiveness initiative confirmed the critical importance of initiating multicultural dialogues and providing inclusive education to all campus members.

THE FACTS ABOUT DIVERSITY INITIATIVES

In one of the only studies of its kind, McCauley, Wright, and Harris (2000) surveyed 281 U.S. 4-year undergraduate institutions on diversity initiatives. They found that 70% of U.S. colleges and institutions offer some form of diversity workshop. Yet only 54% of colleges reported offering diversity training on campus to faculty and staff members. Further, although 54% reported that on-campus staff members were most often the trainers of workshop facilitators, 23% admitted that the facilitators had no formal training on the subject. Not only is there not enough faculty development on diversity issues, but those who do have access to training may be getting inexperienced, unqualified trainers. What kind of results do they report?

In the study by McCauley et al. (2000), 56% of diversity-training respondents saw no positive or negative effects of the workshop on their campus. In spite of this finding, almost all campuses thought their workshops were "worth the time and resources put into it" (p. 107), read: "meaningful." Perhaps they were viewing the diversity initiatives as worthwhile in theory because so many reported that, in practice, the programs had no effect on campus. More disturbing is that 30% of respondents reported that at least one student of color felt hurt by the workshop, and of those, in 75% of the cases, no institutional support or response was provided. Instead, the (possibly untrained) facilitator was expected to respond. Finally, the workshops were not assessed in terms of a change in attitudes or behaviors, so it is impossible to evaluate whether the workshops were effective in terms of real cultural change.

To be prepared for multicultural classrooms, faculty members (as well as other organizational members) need more. They need more training by qualified, experienced, competent staff. It is critical that we look to the literature to learn about best practices to ensure that diversity initiatives will affect positive change to bring about more inclusive educational environments. We also need comprehensive assessment so that we can learn about what works and what doesn't.

Unfortunately, because there are no national standards on diversity, not only are we ignorant as to whether campuses are creating diversity goals, but we also don't know what the goals are or whether and how campuses are meeting those goals. In reality, the goals for each campus could be markedly different. Because campuses are not all the same, some tweaking of a national survey or standard could be considered legitimate, but without any kind of measure (beyond copying another campus's generic, superficial climate survey), each educational institution is forced to reinvent the wheel to create a diversity strategic plan.

THE BENEFITS OF DIVERSITY TRAINING

Owing to the paucity of research specifically on diversity training on campuses (Grant & Secada, 1990; McCauley, Wright, & Harris, 2000; McDonald, 2005), in order to ascertain what works and what doesn't, we must instead turn to the literature on diversity training in the workplace (Bezrukova, Jehn, & Spell, 2012; McCauley, Wright, & Harris, 2000). Pendry, Driscoll, and Field (2007) define diversity training as:

> any discrete programme, or set of programmes, which aims to influence participants to increase their positive—or decrease their negative—intergroup behaviours, such that less prejudice or discrimination is displayed towards others perceived as different in their group affiliation(s). (p. 29)

Many organizations and even business schools start by making the case for multicultural/diversity training. They argue that it contributes to a competitive business advantage. Stevens, Plaut, and Sanchez-Burks (2008) frame diversity training as a stimulus for encouraging constructive growth in an organization, specifically in terms of relationship building across differences, which can strengthen morale and working partnerships. They stress self-affirmation and inclusion of all organization members by viewing intergroup interactions as opportunities for growth and learning rather than as a condition for potential conflict.

Some other benefits of diversity mentioned in the literature include greater creativity and innovation, alternative solutions, harnessing the unique skill sets of diverse individuals, and increasing capacity for workplace collaboration and ingenuity. Diversity training also encourages organization members to serve as role models by accepting and encouraging a variety of opinions and worldviews, which promotes cooperation and teamwork (Bezrukova, Jehn, & Spell, 2012; Chrobot-Mason & Leslie, 2012; Day, 2007; Gonzalez, 2010; McGuire & Bagher, 2010). Furthermore, using a 360-degree feedback instrument, Chrobot-Mason and Leslie (2012) found that multicultural competence correlated with individual job performance, promotion, and overall leadership assessment.

Outcomes of corporate diversity were outlined in a recent article in the *Chicago Sun-Times*. Herring (2013) states that

> racial and gender diversity offers a direct return on investment. It is linked to increased sales revenue, more customers, greater market share, and higher relative profits. Workforce diversity leads to positive business outcomes because growth and innovation depend on people from various backgrounds working together and capitalizing on their differences.

Herring makes the case for diversity on campus as well. Based on his analysis of the National Academy of Sciences Ranking of U.S. Research Universities, he found that academic departments that included more gender and racial diversity received a higher academic ranking, while those departments that were more monocultural were lower in the rankings. Thus, diversity is positively correlated with academic reputation. Just as in corporate culture, diversity provides a direct return on investment in the educational environment. Herring (2013) concludes, "Diversity is an essential ingredient for realizing and keeping a competitive advantage over other educational institutions."

With all the benefits of multicultural education, it would seem that every campus or organization would be willing, if not enthusiastic, about developing diversity initiatives. Unfortunately, this is not the case.

THE CHALLENGES OF DIVERSITY TRAINING

As was true in the aforementioned study by McCauley, Wright, and Harris (2000), some studies have shown diversity training to be not only ineffective at creating inclusiveness, but worse, detrimental. Untrained, inexperienced facilitators are only one of several factors that make diversity-training initiatives challenging. Another is backlash from dominant group members (Kalev, Dobbin, & Kelly, 2006; Mannix & Neale, 2006). Sometimes, dominant group members find a multicultural approach in an organization to be exclusionary (Bendick, Egan, & Lofhjelm, 2001; Plaut, Sanchez-Burks, Buffardi, & Stevens, 2007). Their resistance can take the form of biased language, discrimination, and challenges to diversity policies and practices (Thomas & Plaut, 2008). Moreover, if left unchecked, this discrediting of diversity initiatives can spread and intensify already existing biases against organization members from traditionally marginalized groups (Paluck & Green, 2009; Stevens, Plaut, & Sanchez-Burks, 2008).

Further, diversity training is inherently emotional work. Every individual has a race, a gender, a sexual orientation, a social class, and so forth, and therefore, they come into a workshop with both positive and negative experiences surrounding those identities. More important, they come in with the emotions that are inherently integrated with those experiences. This includes not only those social identities through which they experience some form of bias, discrimination, or oppression (being a person of color, part of the LGBTQ community, and so on), but also those identities that provide them benefits or privilege in society (e.g., being White or heterosexual). Often, participants don't want to be reminded of the ways in which they are more likely to be disadvantaged in society—or of the ways they are likely to receive the benefit of the doubt.

This kind of self-reflection is neither taught nor encouraged in the current educational system, and learning about social inequalities, sometimes for the first time, can challenge previously held beliefs and assumptions. These types of lessons, too, often bring an abundance of emotion. Recent research suggests that learning about the concept of privilege, in particular (including White privilege, heterosexual privilege, male privilege, temporarily able-bodied privilege, among others), can produce feelings of guilt, shame, and general discomfort, especially for members of privileged groups (Adams, Bell, & Griffin, 1997; Allen, 2004; Goodman, 2001; Johnson, 2006; Samuels, 2013b). Of course, that does not mean privilege should not be part of the educational framework of diversity training, but that diversity trainers and educators must understand how participants receive challenging information, the potential discordance they might experience, and the resistance to the diversity-training workshop that might ensue.

For these reasons, multicultural education has often been an issue of compliance when it comes to nondiscrimination laws rather than a proactive approach to create an organization in which every member feels like they belong. In the largest study of its kind, Kalev, Dobbin, and Kelly (2006) surveyed organizations on their diversity initiatives and practices. They concluded that "there are reasons to believe that employers adopt antidiscrimination measures as window dressing, to inoculate themselves against liability, or to improve morale rather than to increase managerial diversity" (p. 610).

If the goal is simply to check a box to comply with federal regulations, then it is likely that the kinds of diversity training being done in many organizations may be doing more harm than good. After all, proficiency in diversity is not a catalog of skills to obtain, but rather a process of education that allows organization members to engage with, respond to, and appreciate members of the organization who have different social group identities from their own (Cox & Beale, 1997). Unfortunately, most often, diversity initiatives are one-time events, lasting less than a day—an item to be checked off a list. Thus, they are rarely incorporated into the policies and practices of an organization, let alone part of a diversity strategic plan (Chrobot-Mason & Quiñones, 2002).

OVERCOMING THE CHALLENGES OF DIVERSITY TRAINING: BEST PRACTICES

Given the multiple challenges to diversity programming and the lack of initiative by many organizations to create a comprehensive plan, how do we know what works? Fortunately, in the corporate world, there are journals and books that have documented and analyzed diversity initiatives at many different organizations, and these have provided recommendations revolving around both the development of an inclusive culture as well as how the organization has fared in the marketplace. Some of these studies and their suggestions are outlined below.

DiversityInc. is one of the leading resources—if not the leading one—on diversity management in the corporate sector, providing rankings of organizations based on each company's diversity policies and practices. Each year, DiversityInc. gathers and analyzes data, and awards the coveted designation of Top 50 Companies for Diversity to those businesses most worthy of the title. It is valuable to learn from DiversityInc.'s analyses because many of the best practices can be applied to college campuses, or to any educational institution.

Madera (2013) studied the best practices used by organizations that have been recognized as top companies in diversity by DiversityInc. Madera found that the top companies incorporated diversity and inclusiveness initiatives into both their policies and practices. Many of those organizations that received a Top 50 award had created formal policies both to increase diversity and decrease discrimination. The success of the organization's diversity policies correlated with the designation of a top executive in the organization to oversee the implementation of the policies, which demonstrates a firm commitment to diversity. Further, these companies provided diversity training, mentoring, and networking programs. Diversity training programs ranged from half a day to a full day, and were offered as often as monthly to employees. Some programs were mandatory and others were not.

Kalev, Dobbin, and Kelly (2006) also found that of the 708 U.S. organizations they surveyed, those that increased racial, ethnic, and gender managerial diversity the most between 1971 and 2002 were those that had established oversight diversity managers, task forces, or committees. These kinds of positions ensure accountability that diversity is incorporated into policy and decisionmaking processes, including hiring decisions. The authors found that oversight practices are more likely to lead to an increase in managerial diversity than diversity-training, networking, or mentoring programs. In fact, the authors found that diversity-training programs result in modest positive effects when a diversity manager is overseeing diversity programming or when some other comparable responsibility/accountability structure is in place.

Linking strategic diversity goals to the organization's vision is another successful strategy (Anand & Winters, 2008). When tied to the larger context of the organization and to the essence of its mission, diversity goals are more likely to be taken seriously and implemented. Among the objectives of the diversity strategy is diversity training. Anand and Winters suggest not only offering workshops to all members of the organization, but also scaffolding courses based on complexity. In other words, once organization members have taken an introductory course, they can then move on to more advanced courses, not only to build awareness of diversity and inclusiveness issues, but also to consider how to practice inclusive behaviors in the workplace.

In their extensive meta-analysis of diversity management practices, Yang and Konrad (2011) found that the organizations that were most effective in terms of their diversity practices were the ones that incorporated a comprehensive strategic diversity plan. Successful campaigns included affinity group formation, specific leadership development activities focusing on recruitment and retention of members of traditionally marginalized groups, targeted marketing campaigns, community outreach, and required diversity training for all managers, among other activities. In addition, they found that ineffective diversity initiatives tended to be those that were isolated and disconnected from a larger strategic plan.

When correlated with employment statistics of women and people of color—specifically, African Americans—the comprehensive strategic plans seem to be at least somewhat effective. Yang and Konrad (2011) add, however, that further research must be undertaken to understand the impact of diversity practices on members of other social groups, including religious groups, LGBTQ, people with disabilities, racial, ethnic, and so on.

Chrobot-Mason and Quiñones (2002) suggest a comprehensive approach to diversity initiatives. Their model includes four components: (1) preparation for diversity training, (2) training development, (3) long-term planning, and (4) evaluation and maintenance. First, preparation incorporates a needs assessment, both of the organization and individuals in it, combined with the creation of training objectives. Second, trainings should include awareness (both of the facts and of one's self), skill building, and action planning (both for the organization and for each individual). Third, planning for effective diversity initiatives entails both ensuring management buy-in and cultivating motivation to learn. Finally, evaluation and maintenance requires the establishment of evaluation criteria and the positive reinforcement of behavioral outcomes. The model brings together a strong organizational commitment to diversity in terms of both policy and cultural change.

Based on their national study of organizations implementing diversity initiatives and organization development theory, Bendick, Egan, and Lofhjelm (2001) developed a list of benchmarks that pinpoint the most successful strategies for diversity training. These include support from top management, training topics and dissemination tailored to the specific group/organization being trained, connection to the broader goals of the organization as a whole, a trainer who works in the same field as the trainees, training for all levels of organization members, training that covers both structural inequalities and individual behavior, and training that is accompanied by analysis of the corporate culture and changes in organizational policies and practices that support what is being taught. Providing opportunities to practice inclusive behavior, perspective taking, role-playing, and intergroup interactions are strongly encouraged (King, Gulick, & Avery, 2010). Experienced and qualified trainers are one of the benchmarks for diversity training outlined by Bendick, Egan, and Lofhjelm (2001).

Chrobot-Mason and Ruderman (2003) suggest a broad range of considerations to enhance multicultural inclusivity. Among them are knowledge of our differences, increased self-awareness, conflict management, interpersonal communication, feedback, role modeling, and a long-term dedication to personal growth and risk-taking. Self-awareness includes a knowledge and critique of one's own biases and assumptions, an understanding of the importance of a commitment to learning about diversity, and perhaps most important, a realization that the commitment is lifelong. Specifically, we are not taught how to interact effectively across our differences, so it is imperative that we seek out the means to continually learn. Further, self-awareness of one's multicultural competence allows us to monitor our own assumptions and behaviors and make adjustments accordingly based on the situation (Chrobot-Mason & Leslie, 2012). The researchers also found a correlation between self-awareness of multicultural competence and others' perception of their success as leaders.

Self-awareness, however, is only one possible goal of diversity training. Research from counseling psychology and Social Identity Development theory views multicultural education as a threefold process: (1) The educator becomes aware of his or her own assumptions, values, and prejudices; (2) the educator engages in learning about the worldviews that are different from their own; and (3) the educator develops specific skills and techniques for building inclusiveness (Sue, Arredondo, & McDavis, 1992). Based on a broad review of the diversity and multicultural competency literature, Chrobot-Mason (2003) found that these three stages of development for an organization can be summed up by increasing awareness, developing behavioral and coping skills, and finally, action planning.

The first phase of training includes not only awareness of personal bias, but also of any institutional structures that serve to discriminate in favor of members of dominant social groups at the expense of members of non-dominant social groups. This could include awareness of those attitudes, behaviors, or policies that make some organization members feel as though they belong, while excluding others.

The second phase of training—developing behavioral and coping skills—entails practicing (through role plays, case studies, or other activities) how to respond and engage in cross-cultural dialogues and conflicts. It takes the *awareness* phase to the next level by applying the knowledge gained in the first phase. It is characterized by flexibility and a willingness/desire to understand others' perspectives.

Finally, the third stage, action planning, brings personal commitment and accountability to the process of building diversity and inclusiveness. It provides participants with the opportunity to consider how they can personally work toward organizational change on an ongoing basis. Research in the field of social psychology has found that making a public commitment to take action increases the likelihood that an individual will follow through with the plan (Cialdini & Goldstein, 2004). Thus, inviting training participants to make a verbal commitment to taking specific steps to build inclusiveness may be an effective strategy. This could be facilitated by asking participants to make a list of actions they plan to take to create inclusiveness, and then going around the room inviting each person to share one or two items on their lists with the group. In addition to increasing their commitment to acting, this process can also ignite ideas in other participants that they may not have thought of before. A few minutes could then be provided for participants to add to their own lists based on new ideas that were sparked when they listened to others' plans.

Moreover, how the commitment is framed can affect an individual's likelihood of carrying out an action. For example, based on self-identity theory, individuals' wish to mold their own identities can actually alter their behavior. For example, asking people if they intend to vote is not as effective in terms of influencing their behavior as asking if they intend to be a voter (Bryan, Walton, Rogers, & Dweck, 2011). In other words, using noun-based wording to describe a desirable social behavior lets people take on the identity of a worthy individual when they eventually perform the behavior. Therefore, asking trainees if they intend to be inclusive educators may be more effective than asking if they intend to educate inclusively. Again, asking for a verbal commitment will increase the likelihood that participants will take action toward this goal/chosen identity.

An action plan can be comprised of both organizational expectations of inclusiveness and specific activities and goals for the organization member to work toward over a specified period of time. This calls for continuous learning, which must be provided by the organization, as well as an individual commitment to engage in cross-cultural relationships both inside and outside of work. Activities might include attending multicultural events in the community, screening and discussing films that focus on multicultural content, and attending multicultural conferences, to name just a few. On an organizational level, an action plan could include benchmarks for the recruitment and retention of organization members from traditionally marginalized groups and, always, a specific plan and a time frame in which to accomplish those goals. (For more ideas and specific activities, see Chrobot-Mason, 2003.)

Applying these principles to campus multicultural training would seem straightforward. However, based on their extensive study of college diversity training, McCauley, Wright, and Harris (2000) did not find it to be as simple as might be expected. First, only 5% of colleges that responded even required faculty to attend diversity workshops, despite the fact that most campuses have a cultural diversity requirement in place for students (Schneider, 2000). Seventy-seven percent of the respondents to McCauley et al.'s survey described the content of the workshop as sharing stories of bias or discrimination. Most said the training included group exercises to explore differences, handouts, personal contact with traditionally marginalized participants, lectures, discussion of campus incidents of bias, role-playing, videos, skits, personality inventories, and case studies.

Although this content might seem to fall into the category of raising awareness, it is not clear whether the discrimination discussed manifests on a personal or structural level. As a result, it may possibly leave out a crucial aspect of training. Moreover, the stories may or may not include recognition of one's own biases, attitudes, and behaviors. Finally, there was neither mention of any kind of action planning, nor any scaffolding for trainings.

EVALUATING CAMPUS DIVERSITY INITIATIVES

Once again, without standards or comprehensive studies on diversity and inclusiveness goals, strategies, and practices on campuses, it is impossible to assess whether any of the initiatives that are currently being implemented are effective. Research on diversity in the workplace, however, provides us with a place to start in terms of figuring out not only what schools and campuses could be doing to increase recruitment and retention of diverse members, but also what questions we should be asking to evaluate diversity initiatives:

1. Does the campus's diversity education incorporate research into practice? In their extensive review of diversity-training research, Roberson, Kulik, and Tan (2013) conclude, "diversity training research should reflect and influence practice, and diversity training practice should reflect and influence research" (p. 359). Evidence shows that most diversity training initiatives are not informed by any specific theoretical framework (Bezrukova, Jehn, & Spell, 2012; Paluck & Green, 2009). Roberson et al. (2013) find a lack of praxis problematic because theory can provide direction and valuable insight into diversity training, and make it more effective.

2. Does the diversity programming provide the opportunity for self-awareness, knowledge of inequalities (both personal and structural), skill building, practicing intercultural interactions, and action planning around inclusiveness? First, as the preparedness model suggests, faculty should be asked to consider the social group memberships of others. Second, they should be asked to reflect on their own identities, biases, and behaviors in order to understand how their attitudes can potentially lead to inclusive or exclusive treatment of others. Third, trainings should include examples of inclusive behavior and the opportunity to practice those behaviors. This serves two purposes: (1) It can increase self-efficacy by demonstrating some of the often minor actions we can take to make a difference, and (2) it can provide specific examples to which educators can connect and perhaps remember the next time they are in a similar situation. Finally, creating an action plan is critical to the efficacy and likelihood that campus members will, in fact, behave inclusively.

Each of these aspects of diversity training must be included for a comprehensive diversity strategic program. They do not all have to occur in one session, but can be implemented in consecutive workshops to be most effective. McCauley et al. (2000) report that most campus diversity trainings were one-time events, with a median length of 2 hours. It is unlikely that all of the above aspects of diversity education could be taught or learned effectively in that brief amount of time; thus, scaffolding is an effective approach.

3. Are the trainings intersectional? Do they focus only on racial differences rather than a myriad of social identities? Holladay, Knight, Paige, and Quiñones (2003) found that backlash from diversity training decreased when a broader approach was used (including several social identities) as opposed to a narrow approach (including only one social identity, such as race or gender). Incorporating an intersectional approach is recommended because it sends the message that everyone is included, which in turn can make participants more likely to accept the precepts of the training (Bezrukova, Jehn, & Spell, 2012; Ely, 2004; Rynes & Rosen, 1995), which would explain why there might be less backlash with such an approach. Moreover, incorporating many different social identities—such as gender, sexuality, disability, and age, in addition to race—in diversity trainings has been shown to decrease the typically intense, and often unwanted, focus on participants of color by broadening the spectrum of bias and discrimination that exists on most campuses and in most schools today (Samuels, 2013b).

4. Are workshops facilitated by experienced, trained diversity professionals? Of the colleges surveyed by McCauley, Wright, and Harris (2000), only 32% used a diversity consultant, 72% said that most often college staff members were the facilitators of their workshops, and 41% reported that faculty members were the facilitators. Thirty-seven percent of respondents claimed that diversity workshop facilitators were trained by off-campus professionals, while 23% admitted that the facilitators had no formal training at all.

Roberson, Kulik, and Tan (2013) assert that a lack of experienced trainers can unintentionally accentuate and solidify differences between social groups, leading to negative consequences. Moreover, inexperienced trainers may not be equipped to handle the emotional component of diversity training, causing a loss in credibility that may be unrecoverable. This can render trainings not only useless, but worse, can also cause cynicism and mistrust not only about diversity training, but also about the organization in general (Arredondo, 1996; Paluck & Green, 2009).

Further, as previously stated, inexperienced or untrained/poorly trained instructors can sometimes, even unintentionally, bring their own biases into a workshop. They may be teaching multicultural values while simultaneously modeling biased behavior. A lack of behavioral integrity can cause participants to reject the entire premise of the training (Simons, 2002).

5. Are the diversity programs voluntary? Although mandatory diversity training demonstrates a commitment to inclusiveness on an institutional level (Kellough & Naff, 2004; Rynes & Rosen, 1995), research shows that those who are forced to participate may not benefit from it (Dobbin, Kalev, & Kelly, 2007; Paluck, 2006; van Dick et al., 2004). In fact, mandated training can have negative repercussions, including but not limited to resistance to the topics being presented. Voluntary training, on the other hand, can lead to more diversity in management-level positions (Dobbin & Kalev, 2007). Furthermore, tying diversity and inclusiveness training to tenure, raises, and promotion in schools and on campuses would go a long way toward ensuring that faculty members would get the education they need to create and maintain an inclusive campus environment. Institutionalizing such training programs and devoting funds to the education of the trainers would represent positive steps toward accountability and performance standards, and would send a strong message from the administrators of the educational institution that diversity is a value worth embracing (King, Gulick, & Avery, 2010).

6. Are the diversity trainings being assessed as to their effectiveness (specifically, increasing the likelihood that campus members will, in fact, behave inclusively)? Despite more than 450 articles focusing on diversity in the workplace since 2000, there is almost no thorough analysis or evaluation of diversity training in the literature (Anand & Winters, 2008; Ivancevich & Gilbert, 2000; Paluck & Green, 2009; Stevens, Plaut, & Sanchez-Burks, 2008). Lack of evaluation means a lack of accountability, not only for the trainings and the trainers, but also for the members of the organization (Chrobot-Mason & Quiñones, 2002).

Chrobot-Mason (2003) notes that what little assessment of diversity training has been conducted has been based on the self-report of participants. She suggests that a full evaluation of training would not only incorporate self-reports, but also the assessment of particular organization members' inclusive behaviors before and after the training by other organization members. This feedback loop would demonstrate an institutional commitment to inclusiveness.

7. If the answer to any of these questions is no, then are the funds and time devoted to these diversity and inclusiveness endeavors worthwhile? As Hurtado (1992) and Milem (1994) assert, faculty members have a strong part to play in the process of building an inclusive environment. The answers to the above questions could have a strong impact on the recruitment and retention of diverse campus members, which remains a tremendous challenge in schools and on campuses across the United States.

OTHER EFFECTIVE INCLUSIVENESS SOLUTIONS

Social Identity Development (SID)

Are the trainers of diversity workshops considering the Social Identity Development (SID) of participants? The varying levels/stages that participants are in can increase or decrease their willingness to engage in the training, and might lead to resistance to the material presented. Chrobot-Mason and Quiñones (2002) suggest conducting a pretraining personal analysis of organization members. Members are provided with a SID model such as Bennett's Developmental Model of Intercultural Sensitivity (1986) or Hardiman and Jackson's (1997) SID model, and they are invited to figure out where in the model they fit. This activity is useful in several ways. First, in preparation for the training, it provides trainers with valuable information about how to differentiate diversity training (e.g., awareness-based training for some; skill-building training and action planning for others). Second, it gives trainers insight into participants' potential sources of resistance to diversity materials.

Third, the activity not only provides members with an understanding of their own level of development, but also pinpoints the goals and diversity expectations of the organization (which should correlate to the more advanced levels/stages on whichever model is used). In other words, it highlights for organization members where they are and where they need to be. And finally, once they become more aware of the cultural expectations toward which the organization is working, members may be more receptive to, and even eager about, the upcoming training, because they understand that they may not be as far along as they need to be, and must learn the information and skills the training offers in order to succeed in the organization.

Implicit Association Test (IAT)

Another useful strategy hails from the research of Ashburn-Nardo, Morris, and Goodwin (2008). These researchers suggest having organization members take Harvard University's Implicit Association Test (IAT) to become aware of their own subtle forms of bias. Taking the IAT is an easy way to raise awareness for diversity education. The next step, these authors suggest, is to raise awareness on the gravity of discrimination in terms of both short- and long-term consequences. If organization members are made to understand bias and inequality as an emergency, it could give them efficacy to act. Next would be to set an expectation within the organization from the highest levels that offensive comments or behavior will not be tolerated, and to encourage organization members to take responsibility for intervening in these types of microaggressions. Finally, skill building and action planning would include teaching organization members how to intervene or confront an offender, and providing opportunities for them to practice those interventions through case studies or role-playing. Czopp (2007) found that after witnessing a successful confrontation, subjects were more likely to intervene themselves when they encountered racist behavior.

All-Inclusive Multiculturalism (AIM)

Stevens, Plaut, and Sanchez-Burks (2008) recommend using what they call the AIM model (All-Inclusive Multiculturalism). They found a positive effect when they explicitly stated that diversity includes *all* organization members, rather than only members of traditionally marginalized groups. Individuals had a more inclusive implicit association with the idea of diversity and multiculturalism than did individuals who did not receive that message. Similar results were found in other studies—specifically, that focusing on similarities rather than differences in diversity training correlated with less backlash (Bezrukova, Jehn, & Spell, 2012) and more effective conflict resolution (Holladay & Quiñones, 2008). Focusing on inclusiveness in this way might translate to less bias between groups and a greater likelihood for building relationships across difference.

eTraining

Some scholars suggest using technology to offer diversity-training scenarios. They are pushing well past the idea of showing a video clip and moving into the realm of diversity training through etraining, webinars, and videogaming (Anand & Winters, 2008). Some organizations are even using SecondLife technology to emulate diversity situations. Participants use avatars to interact with each other in a three-dimensional immersive social environment. In this structure, they can learn about and even experience different worlds and cultures. The benefits of these kinds of technological trainings is that they can be offered anywhere in the world. The ease of access and cost-effectiveness is appealing to some organizations. In addition, scaffolding courses or scenarios into more and more challenging situations is feasible, and diversity and inclusiveness can be integrated into any training in this way.

These kinds of trainings might be useful for increasing awareness and practicing skills, but in the relatively limited contact that one avatar has with another (as opposed to in real life), they may not be effective for learning how to build complex relationships across difference (one of the main goals of diversity training, and one of the final stages in most SID models). More specifically, etraining could be problematic because of contact hypothesis: that bias between two groups can be reduced through the interaction between the groups (Pettigrew & Tropp, 2006). Without real-life contact, the effectiveness of the training is questionable. That said, some organizations are choosing to use a combination of etraining and classroom/workshop contact. More research and assessment is needed in this area to evaluate these kinds of programs (Anand & Winters, 2008).

Overall, this last point applies to all campus diversity strategic initiatives. Without a comprehensive plan, thorough implementation overseen by campus leadership, and measurable outcomes that are tracked and analyzed, we will continue to spend money, time, and resources on initiatives that may not meet the needs of all of our education stakeholders: campus members, the larger community, the nation, and ultimately, the globe. In fact, Anand and Winters (2008) predict that diversity training must soon be led by those who have specific expertise in cultural differences across the world. If this is the future of diversity training, we are already lagging behind.

Employee Resource Groups (ERGs)

DiversityInc., the organization that annually identifies the top 50 U.S. organizations that are most effective in their diversity and inclusiveness practices, finds that more and more top diversity organizations are creating Employee Resource Groups (ERGs). In the past, these groups were called affinity or networking groups, but now they are called ERGs in order to emphasize their role as an important resource to the company and not a social group or a place simply to complain. Frankel (2009) reports that successful ERGs include a senior staff person who does not run the group but who can liaise with the administration. This person, ideally, is not a member of the social identity of the group, but rather an ally to the group. So, for example, the senior staff of an LGBTQ ERG would ideally be someone who is heterosexual. This shows organizational support for the ERG without making it what some may call a "special interest" group.

All ERGs should be open to anyone because cross-cultural participation builds understanding, education, and relationships across difference. The administration meets with each ERG regularly for those same reasons. And finally, Frankel adds that the groups are often marketed internally and participation is encouraged. Then, once they are running smoothly, they can be used to recruit more members of a particular social identity using specific community awareness and understanding. By 2009, all top 50 organizations had an LGBTQ ERG, 92% had an ERG around disability, and 26% included an ERG for veterans. ERGs in other areas (religious, younger workers, older workers, global issues, and so forth) are continuing to grow. Among their many benefits are increased recruitment and retention of members of traditionally marginalized groups, mentoring, and talent development. There is ample reason to believe that ERGs for faculty and staff could be just as beneficial.

In fact, all of the diversity and inclusiveness initiatives mentioned can be used on any campus or in any school. Cultural inclusiveness mandates that we take action, and these strategies can lead to a comprehensive diversity plan. Once the training is achieved, the next step in building cultural inclusiveness is to consider how we implement inclusive practices.

CHAPTER 4

Building Culturally Inclusive Classrooms

> Education can change culture but only in so far as educators are transformed.
>
> —*Parent School Board USA*

During a recent visit to a well-known and well-respected Ivy League university in the northeastern United States to which my daughter was considering applying, we were escorted into a great hall for the standard information session before the campus walking tour. As I walked into the hall, I was immediately struck by the choice the university made to usher prospective students into this particular gallery. The walls were lined with colossal portraits, each of which ran from the floor to the three-story ceiling, displaying every president in the history of the university. Every single one was a White male.

I couldn't help but consider what message the university was sending to prospective students who entered the room, as they were dwarfed by the humongous images staring down at them. Did the admissions office consider how this specific choice of rooms would impact students? What underlying message were they sending, not only to the previously eager students of color, but also to White students, about their chances of belonging at this university? And by extension, what kind of education would students receive in an institution where the administration demonstrated such a sense of self-import, with an apparent expectation that they should be revered almost as gods? I considered how many thousands of students might apply to the institution based on its reputation alone, but wondered what their educational experience would teach them, if they were accepted, about the growing multicultural world in which we live.

TRADITIONAL CLASSROOMS

In the 20th century, at this Ivy League university and at most K–20 educational institutions, the typical classroom was a space where teachers or professors would stand in the front of the room pontificating with the hope that their vast knowledge would be received and comprehended by their students (Moore, 2005; O'Malley & McCraw, 1999). Students would then be asked to regurgitate the knowledge in the form of a written test, which was often standardized (Kohn, 2000). Using over a century of data, Cuban (1993) describes traditional classroom practice as largely teacher-centered. In other words, teachers do most of the talking, there is little to no differentiated instruction so the teacher instructs the whole class at once, the teacher decides how to spend class time (relying largely on the textbook to structure the curriculum), and classrooms are arranged in such a way that the teacher is in front looking out at rows of desks.

Although this framework is still being used in many educational institutions across the nation, over the past few decades, traditional instruction has been critiqued as a form of education that invites passive learning and disregards the individual needs of students (Hannum & Briggs, 1982). Its prevalence has continued primarily because it is most likely that teachers themselves were taught this way and so they perpetuate the same model of instruction (Kohn, 2000). In contrast, Moore (2005) suggests, "An enormous potential exists for universities to be leaders in questioning the status quo, challenging paradigms and openly practicing new ways of living, thinking, teaching, and learning" (p. 78).

NONTRADITIONAL CLASSROOMS

A more contemporary approach to classroom structure is student-centered curricula. As opposed to teacher-centered curricula, this approach allows students to make decisions about what is taught, how it is taught, and how the room is set up to best accommodate the needs of all students. In this case, students talk as much as if not more than the teacher, differentiated learning occurs either individually or in small groups, and students participate in determining some, if not all, of the norms or expected behaviors in the classroom (Cuban, 1993). Based on the idea that learning is an active process, in a nontraditional classroom, students are encouraged to take an active part in their learning through engagement and collaboration with both their teacher and their classmates (Kohn, 2000). Assessment is multifaceted. Rather than simply relying on written tests to evaluate a student's retention of facts, intentional learning environments incorporate performance, projects, portfolios, and the application of knowledge (Brown, 1992).

In a nontraditional classroom, educators are expected to be responsive to students' needs and questions rather than teaching a fixed curriculum in a specified time frame. Flexibility is encouraged and even required (Brown,

1992). Not all educators welcome this approach. It requires more from them than just learning their subject matter; they must be willing and able to learn how to effectively facilitate a more dynamic classroom environment, which can be unpredictable.

Those educators and policymakers who critique a nontraditional approach tend to question new theories of education based primarily on the fact that they are new, rather than using concrete evidence to challenge their value in the classroom (Chall, 2000). In fact, a myriad of positive outcomes are outlined in the literature. For example, far from focusing only on the individual's attainment of knowledge, collaborative learning brings diverse students together to work toward a common goal. Students are responsible for one another's attainment of the material as well as their own. Student success is based in part on the ability to engage with a community of learners (Gokhale, 1995). The focus is on the exchange of experiences and ideas, and the goal is a common understanding based on the cocreation of knowledge by the students (Cranton, 1996; Nieto, 1999). This type of learning heightens interest in the subject matter and promotes critical thinking and the exchange of ideas (Gokhale, 1995).

TRANSFORMATIVE LEARNING

Freire and Macedo (1995) offer a form of student-focused teaching that engages students in self-reflection and empowers them to become social agents of change in society. Emancipatory transformative learning includes relationship building between teacher and student using dialogical methodology based on mutual respect. Transformative Learning (TL) has been shown to actually alter brain structure and develop neural pathways because it centers on curiosity, engages students' interests, and makes use of emotional, perceptional, and kinesthetic methodology (Janik, 2005). Moreover, Mezirow (1996) suggests that TL (as opposed to traditional learning) leads to "a more fully developed (more functional) frame of reference . . . one that is more (a) inclusive, (b) differentiating, (c) permeable, (d) critically reflective, and (e) integrative of experience" (p. 163). Positive outcomes of TL include an increase in self-confidence, self-efficacy, spiritual growth, compassion for others, creativity, new relationships, and changes in the ways one interacts with others (Taylor, 1997).

More Benefits of Transformative Learning

TL offers a student-centered approach for the future. It bridges individuals and larger social structures by taking into consideration one's social identities and how those identities impact our lives. Cross-cultural awareness and relationships facilitate transformative learning. Culturally responsive strategies include storytelling and group inquiry, and position the teacher as collaborator rather than expert in the learning process (Taylor, 2008). TL is often political in that it challenges dominant hierarchical thinking. In a non-Eurocentric context, it allows for cultural inclusion (providing a space for traditionally marginalized voices), promotes enfranchisement, and builds communication and engagement across cultures (Taylor, 2008). Moreover, unlike traditional instruction, TL paves the way for individual and social change through the establishment of collective goals within the learning community (Cranton, 1996).

Additionally, TL incorporates the global concept of sustainability. It emphasizes a connection between the individual and the planet by considering not only our natural environment and the need to protect it, but also the larger human community. It calls for a radical shift in educational theory and practices to begin to ameliorate the ecological crisis we are in. Moore (2005) explains, "The concept [of sustainability] speaks to the reconciliation of social justice, ecological integrity, and the well-being of all living systems on the planet" (p. 78). She adds, "Sustainability education must be interdisciplinary, collaborative, experiential, and potentially transformative. . . . [It] is also a process of creating a space for inquiry, dialogue, reflection, and action about the concept and goals of sustainability" (p. 78). Social action is a critical component of sustainability education and TL in terms of making a difference both on a personal and societal level (Taylor, 2008).

Teaching with a TL lens integrates the whole person in the classroom. In other words, rather than leaving one's emotions, spirituality, social identities, personal experiences, and so on outside, TL takes a holistic approach (Dirkx, 2006). Moreover, central to TL is critical reflection that encourages learners to challenge their own biases and assumptions and to engage in perspective taking (Moore, 2005). This creates an interesting challenge for educators who are then required to gain knowledge and experience in managing emotions and ensuring civilized behavior in the classroom, if they want to be successful. Educators can facilitate TL by offering experiences for learners to engage in critical reflection through journaling and dialogue, for example, and to practice and apply the new perspectives they have learned. Without practice, full transformation for students is unlikely (Taylor, 2008).

Most important, in order to be effective using a transformational approach, educators must undertake their own processes of self-reflection and transformation (Johnson-Bailey & Alfred, 2006; Moore, 2005). TL provides an opportunity for educators to grow and transform themselves. As Taylor (2008) concludes:

> It means asking yourself, Am I willing to transform in the process of helping my students transform? This means taking the position that without developing a deeper awareness of our own frames of reference and how they shape practice, there is little likelihood that we can foster change in others. (p. 13)

Educators who choose to utilize a TL approach can facilitate students' social justice journey and even encourage them to take personal and/or social action, but what that action is must be left up to the student. If it is not, the teaching methodology could resemble indoctrination (Cranton, 1994).

Challenges of Transformative Learning

TL may not be the best approach for every educator. Its complexity demands a fair amount of time and energy not only to learn best TL practices, but also to implement new ideas and new ways of thinking about the construction and sharing of knowledge. It also compels educators to dedicate themselves to a lifelong learning process, and to acquire a willingness to make mistakes and try again.

It also requires support. Throughout this process, it is critical for students and faculty to get the support they need to go through a transformative learning experience. It is difficult to accomplish with support; without support, it is impossible. With the many challenges TL brings, both personal and collegiate support networks are essential (Moore, 2005). As Kohli (2008) states, a social justice approach "is a difficult and uphill battle, but the more that we believe in the immense value of diverse cultural knowledge, language and rich traditions, the more equipped we will be to create spaces that educate and empower" (p. 187).

Additionally, not every student may be comfortable in a TL classroom. Some students prefer to learn in a more anonymous environment where they are not required to direct their own learning, reflect on their own attitudes and behaviors, or come up with creative questions (Moore, 2005). Furthermore, the time and energy dedicated to TL practices may not be well received by institutions that don't value risk-taking in the classroom or nontraditional teaching practices (Cranton, 1996). On the other hand, if the goal is to create an inclusive classroom where all students and their ideas are welcomed, respected, and encouraged, then the benefits of TL far outweigh the challenges.

Time for Change

The time and effort required by both students and faculty would inexorably transform the educational system because all stakeholders would have even more of a vested interest in how and what they are dedicating themselves to. It is clear that we need a change. Too many students are (feeling) alienated in the classroom. It is important to note that old-fashioned skills-based instruction is more likely to be the standard in schools comprised mostly of students of color from low-income families. It is difficult to accurately compare that kind of education with the more progressive education that includes higher-order thinking that mostly wealthy, White students are receiving in more affluent public and private schools (Kohn, 2000). TL offers a different kind of classroom for everyone and has the potential of leveling the playing field of education by respecting the various learning styles and needs of every single student.

Furthermore, although discomfort is not unusual in TL and might be difficult for students and faculty members to navigate, we might consider the larger question: What is an education for? If students and faculty stay within their comfort zones, how much are they really learning, thinking, and growing? That is not to say that class members must be uncomfortable throughout their educational experience; rather, I suggest that comfort in the classroom is overrated. Leaning in to the discomfort instead of away from it can be transformative. This is where real growth can happen.

TRANSFORMING THE CURRICULUM

Culturally inclusive classrooms don't just come about when multicultural students or faculty step into the room. I like to think of inclusiveness as a verb. It takes a commitment to learn strategies that will make every student feel like they belong and can succeed. Gorski (2010) provides a list of suggestions for becoming a better multicultural educator. Among these are learning to pronounce each student's full name accurately, scrutinizing all course materials to make sure they are free from bias (and challenging them with the class when they are not), soliciting anonymous feedback from students and taking their critiques seriously, and taking personal responsibility for those students who are not succeeding in class to see how systems of oppression might be contributing to their falling behind.

Further, he suggests teaching about multicultural issues (racism, sexism, heterosexism, poverty, and so forth) at the earliest possible level because many students are already experiencing the effects of discrimination and oppression in their lives at very young ages. Overall, learning happens best when students are offered a challenge; are told that they can, in fact, navigate and overcome the challenge; and when a sense of interest of the material is cultivated so that students want to continue to learn about the topic (Malone & Lepper, 1987; Zeichner, 1992). When students are given specific, short-term objectives, and have the efficacy that they can accomplish the task and a willingness to do so, they are more likely to succeed (Schunk, 1989).

Most of all, culturally inclusive curriculum requires educators to reflect on their own teaching practices, and to consider the following questions.

1. Do I use a variety of teaching strategies to accommodate diverse learning styles? How students learn is a complex question—one that has been studied in many fields, including education, developmental psychology, anthropology, and sociology, among others. The comprehensive research of Dunn and Dunn (1979) produced four categories to consider when thinking about how students learn best. These ranged from environmental elements (sound, light, temperature, and classroom design) to emotional elements (motivation, persistence, responsibility, need for structure), to sociological elements (working alone or in groups), to physical elements (perceptual strengths, time of day). Further, they found that only between 20 and 30% of students are auditory, while 40% are visual, and the rest are kinesthetic, visual/kinesthetic, or some other combination of senses. These findings suggest that only between 20 and 30% of students are likely to succeed in a lecture-style classroom.

Moreover, educators typically teach the way they learn best (Dunn & Dunn, 1979). As a result, there can be mismatch between teaching methodology and learning. As Grasha and Yangarber-Hicks (2000) explain, "any instructional process that tries to shape how we learn or teach will either encourage and reinforce our preferred styles, or create pressures for us to modify them" (p. 3). Scholars have found that when teaching and learning styles are matched, increases in both student achievement and motivation occur (Cropper, 1994; Dunn & Dunn, 1979). Thus, it is incumbent on educators to reflect on their own learning style(s) and to learn strategies and techniques that work best for students whose learning styles differ from their own.

One example of this potential mismatch is on the basis of introversion/extroversion. If a lead educator is an extrovert (someone who gains energy from engaging in groups), they may not consider the potentially significant challenges experienced in class by an introvert (someone who gains energy from being alone). An extrovert may not see a problem with assessing students based on their class participation; however, doing so could ultimately privilege extroverts over introverts.

Using more inclusive strategies can minimize this problem. One way to encourage everyone's participation is to include journaling as part of the class experience. Asking a specific question, or asking students to reflect on class material, regardless of the subject matter, gives all students the opportunity and the time to consider their response. Once they have written their response, they can even be divided into dyads or triads to practice sharing the responses they wrote. Finally, when the class comes back together as a group, students who do not typically share are invited to do so. Anecdotally, I have found that students are much more likely to share once these added steps have been offered, and moreover, they do so with confidence. This strategy also works well for students who need extra time to process material before they are able to participate in class (Samuels, 2009c).

In consideration of all students, including those who have a disability, a culturally inclusive practice is to incorporate the principles of Universal Design for Learning (UDL). The legal objective of universal design is to provide goods and services that can be utilized by people with the broadest array of functional capabilities (Edyburn, 2010). Many education scholars and activists consider UDL beneficial not just for people with disabilities, but also for everyone (King-Sears, 2009). For example, in terms of a physical building, ramps are useful not only for people who use wheelchairs as a means of transport, but also for delivery carts. Another example is an easy accommodation that would change all gender-specified bathrooms to gender-neutral or nonspecified, especially if they are single-stall bathrooms. It is simple to change the plaque outside the bathroom to simply say "restroom" rather than have it indicate a gendered space. This is inclusive not only for transgender individuals and gender nonconforming individuals, but also makes it so that no one has to wait to use a restroom until the specific gendered bathroom is available.

Universal Instructional Design (UID) (Silver, Bourke, & Strehorn, 1998) goes one step further to provide specific pedagogical practices for educators who choose to make their classrooms more student-focused and inclusive for all (Hackman, 2008). Based on the inclusiveness practices outlined by Chickering and Gamson (1987), UID incorporates several elements for creating an inclusive classroom. They include creating a respectful classroom climate, providing well-defined expectations and feedback, using a variety of teaching techniques and assessment methods, utilizing technology to enrich learning, and fostering interaction between faculty and students (Fox, Hatfield, & Collins, 2003).

In order to accomplish these goals, the University of Minnesota's Curriculum Transformation and Disability project recommends that faculty development training incorporate UID into their curricula. The training encourages educators to:

> (a) build on their own experiences, (b) learn about relevant legislation, (c) become familiar with and begin to apply the principles of Universal Instructional Design, (d) identify specific ways to create inclusive classrooms and programs,

> (e) learn about assistive technology, (f) learn about local resources, and (g) develop a personal action plan. (Fox, Hatfield, & Collins, 2003, pp. 23–26)

UID requires that teachers learn about the students in their classrooms so they can best match their learning styles to become more successful. For example, activating the subtitles in conjunction with the volume when showing a media clip benefits not only people who have an auditory disability, but also provides visual learners with another means of acquiring the material presented. Although UID requires advance planning, "faculty members who endeavor to implement UID find that it can be liberating, enabling them to bring more creativity to their teaching, and also rewarding, because students are responsive to more inclusive pedagogy" (Higbee, Chung, & Hsu, 2004, p. 23).

2. Do the materials I use in my courses help students understand historical, social, and/or political events from diverse perspectives? McCutcheon (1982) explains that curriculum is "what students have an opportunity to learn . . . through both the hidden and overt curriculum, and what they do not have an opportunity to learn because certain matters were not included" (p. 19). Reviewing curricula from an inclusiveness lens makes it abundantly clear that the education that most students (and faculty, for that matter) have received is based largely on one perspective of history.

In the process of creating textbooks, although academics often have a multiplicity of meanings, definitions, and perspectives from which to choose, teachers have fewer from which to choose, and typically, students are provided the opportunity to learn only one (Cherryholmes, 1988). Sleeter and Grant (2010) state that this reductive process

> legitimates existing social relations and the status of those who dominate, and it does so in a way that implies that there are no alternative versions of the world, and that the interpretation being taught in schools is, indeed, undisputed fact. (p. 186)

This monocultural lens has been hailed by former secretary of education William Bennett, among others, who have called for a substantial *increase* in the study of the "Great Books" and Western culture. Going in this direction not only ignores diversity and equity issues, but also is redundant with the materials that are currently taught. In 1987, Bloom echoed this call for more traditional teachings in his book entitled *The Closing of the American Mind*. Bloom's book became a number-one *New York Times* bestseller, has sold more than a million copies, and recently printed a 25th-anniversary edition. Rather than what he likely meant to be a rallying cry, the title of Bloom's book seems to reflect his prescription for the educational system.

These ideas are pervasive, and serve to provide a myopic perspective of the world where some voices are heard while others are silenced. And the situation does not seem to be improving. Based on their extensive research of textbooks, Sleeter and Grant (2010) found that in the past few decades, there has not been much headway made in the handling of diversity in textbooks. In fact, there seems to be growing momentum toward more White- and male-dominated curricula. We need instead to be asking these questions in *every* subject, regardless of which course materials we use: Whose voice is being heard in this material? Whose voices are missing or being misrepresented?

We also need more books like James Loewen's *Lies My Teacher Told Me: Everything Your American History Textbook Got Wrong* and Howard Zinn's *A People's History of the United States: 1492 to Present*. These books offer a historic representation of the United States from diverse perspectives that are typically left out of history classes. Not only do books like these offer a diversion from the standard curriculum, but they also serve to challenge the pervasive hegemonic discourse, allowing students the opportunity to broaden their own perspectives. Most important, learning from a broader curriculum gives all students the opportunity to reflect on what they have been taught and to consider what has been missing from their education.

3. Are the texts/readings I use written by authors from diverse backgrounds (different races, sexual orientations, genders, abilities, and so on)? Do I draw references and examples from different cultural groups in my classes, regardless of the topic I teach? No matter the subject matter, it is imperative that students see themselves reflected in the course materials (Gay, 2000). Once again, a multiplicity of ideas, content, social movements, and so forth can bring students in, engage them, and provide them with the opportunity to think and learn beyond the boundaries that have been traditionally dictated in the classroom. Bringing the social identities of the authors of course materials to the forefront whenever possible makes the authors more real and more relatable. In addition, including authors whose social identities are nondominant teaches students about differences and allows them to consider how those identities (much like their own) might impact how and what the authors choose to write. Moreover, learning about the contributions of scholars, scientists, mathematicians, and others from traditionally marginalized groups can be empowering to all students. Thus, this conversation can be part of any class discussion, no matter what subject is being taught.

Unfortunately, these kinds of conversations do not happen very frequently. Too often, diversity is an afterthought or is taught only during certain months that correspond to specific holidays (Anti-Defamation League, 2005). As Pettis-Renwick (2002) laments, "the central problem lies in the way we have traditionally chosen to incorporate diverse peoples and perspectives into the curriculum—as adjuncts to the main story rather than as a central part of the story itself" (p. 37). She adds, "Mentioning only famous individuals ignores the true panorama of human life. Studying events that are important to different groups, and examining their worldviews and contributions" (p. 37) is critically important to students' full understanding of our world. Further, incorporating authors and materials from diverse cultures serves to benefit all students. Gay (1997) explicates, "The lives of the citizens of the United States, individually and collectively, are inextricably interrelated and what happens to one invariably affects the other" (p. 5). This is an integral lesson for all students to learn in a growing multicultural world.

4. Do I assign projects that enable students from diverse groups to work together both collaboratively and effectively? Traditionally, students were expected to learn on their own, in isolation, responsible for their own achievements. The underlying message was that in a competitive world, it is incumbent on the individual to work harder than anyone else to get ahead. In response to our increasingly global culture, this message warrants more critical consideration. What skills will future citizens need? Certainly, learning about social differences and how best to collaborate across those differences is an essential component of a contemporary education. In fact, this idea is corroborated by social learning theory (Vygotsky, 1978), which affirms that active involvement and the exchange of ideas with others are crucial to learning. Moreover, collaborative learning has been found to increase student performance and help students develop deeper relationships with their peers (Drouin, 2010).

Many innovative community-learning strategies are being used in K–20 classrooms to accomplish this goal. One example is *reciprocal teaching* (Brown & Campione, 2002). This approach gives students the opportunity to be both learners and learning leaders. The learning leader asks questions of the other students and/or the teacher to facilitate comprehension of course material, and encourages other students to ask questions, too. The method demands student engagement and interaction in the learning process. For this approach to be effective, the teacher monitors the interactions, pushes students toward a more complex understanding of the material, remains quiet whenever the students are able to take responsibility for their own learning, and clarifies the steps taken in the class's progress with the material. The teacher's role in outlining the class's learning journey serves a dual purpose: It provides the opportunity for students to better understand the learning process and the repetition allows those students who need it some extra time to grasp the material.

Another example of community learning that has been around for a few decades and is still relevant is the Jigsaw method (Aronson, 1978). Subject matter is divided into five subtopics; students are then divided into five research groups. Each research group is responsible for learning about their subtopic and creating a presentation for teaching their subtopic. This entails reading, research, writing, analyzing, and so on, and encourages enthusiastic participation, especially because students are aware that they will need to present their subtopic, so they will need to become veritable experts on it. Subsequently, students regroup into learning groups made up of one student from each of the five subtopics. Coming together like a jigsaw puzzle in the learning groups, each student is responsible for teaching the rest of the group about their subtopic in an interactive, engaging way, at whatever level they are able. The learning groups allow students to practice their teaching and facilitation skills, leading discussion, answering questions, and truly engaging their peers (Brown & Campione, 2002). The more the students are aware of the fact that different students learn differently, the more creative and inclusive their presentations will be, which can be beneficial for all.

5. Do I enable students to demonstrate knowledge in multiple ways that reflect diverse learning styles? Traditionally, assessment has been based on an individual's achievement on written examinations and papers. A more inclusive approach would be to offer students alternatives. Kitano (1996) suggests that teachers provide students the opportunity to apply what they have learned through action-oriented projects, portfolios, and other creative assignments. Counting a self-assessment in a student's grade can be useful so that students have the chance to reflect on their own contribution to the learning community (Black & Wiliam, 1998). Using an essay format with prompts, students can assess their own performance and what they could have done better. (For more information on variations of providing students with feedback, see Wininger, 2005.)

As opposed to strictly objectively knowing the material, students can be challenged to make sense of materials, also adding the ability to apply what they are learning. In addition, grading rubrics for projects and presentations can incorporate multicultural principles to encourage students to think and research critically. They can be evaluated on how inclusive their presentation is of nondominant cultures. They can be graded on how effectively they researched the events and experiences of peoples of traditionally marginalized groups, for example, rather than presenting only on the traditional curricula.

Further, inclusive assessment practices can take the form of a group quiz retake. First, each student individually takes an objective-style quiz (multiple choice, matching, and so on). Before scoring those quizzes, students are divided into groups, and each group receives a blank quiz to take together. Group members are asked to discuss each question and to teach one another what they have learned. Once they have completed the quiz together, each group turns in their group quiz (S. Samuels, personal communication, January 5, 2014). On a study of group-based exams, Drouin (2010) found that after a 5-week individual retest, students who had completed the group quiz activity 5 weeks prior scored an average of 10% higher than their original individual scores. In the meantime, students who had worked only individually increased their 5-week retest scores by a mere 1%. These are some examples of creative ways to expand our assessment practices to make them more inclusive.

6. Do I make my cultural inclusiveness transparent to students? Kitano (1997) recommends providing a statement on the syllabus and/or online about the importance of a multicultural approach. Such a statement accomplishes several tasks. First, it lets all students know that the faculty member accepts, appreciates, and welcomes every student into the class. Second, it sets the tone for the class in terms of what kinds of language and behavior will be expected. Third, it informs students that the course will be inclusive, based on multicultural principles, rather than a traditional-style classroom.

Altman and Cashin (1992) suggest providing resource information for learning centers on campus. This not only tells students that these are important references, but also that there is a variety of ways that they can increase their success as students. Reminding students of these resources, and other pertinent syllabus information, throughout the course makes it more likely that students will abide by the syllabus as a contract between educator and student, and make more use of the resources provided (Becker & Calhoon, 1999). Aside from support services, plagiarism statements, and other information, it is useful to include the diversity/inclusiveness statement of the institution (if there is one) to demonstrate, once again, the importance of this information. Additionally, students often do not know they have recourse when exclusion happens on campus; thus, a syllabus can outline the process students can initiate if they or someone they know experiences exclusion, including the contact information for the ombuds office or other administrative office in charge of such complaints. This empowers students to know and to act, if and when necessary.

TRANSFORMING THE CLASSROOM

Physical Space

Another way to make room for transformative growth is to consider the physical space of the classroom. As opposed to the traditional setting of desks in rows, which tends to isolate students, in more progressive classrooms, desks are set up in clusters or in one large circle where students are given the opportunity to work in groups, with a partner, and/or as a community. This allows for a myriad of learning styles, and challenges the old notion of competition and learning by rote. It also provides the opportunity for students to build relationships and learn to work together with peers who have different social identities from their own.

Name tents are another method of fostering relationships. Card stock or extra-large index cards folded in half make excellent name tents. Students write their names on the front and back of the tent to accommodate not only those students who are sitting across the room from them, but also the ones sitting next to them. Being able to see one another and one another's names gives the immediate impression that this space is different from other classroom environments. It is an effective way to immediately break down barriers between students, and lets them know that they will not only be learning from the materials and the lead educator, but also from one another. Students often remark at how these techniques helped them feel more comfortable to participate in class (Samuels, 2009c).

Classroom Engagement

To encourage participation, community expectations/norms are useful. Creating a community engagement agreement is especially important in a class that encourages discussion so that all class members are clear about what is expected of them. There is a variety of ways to create this contract with students. One is to provide students with a few suggested norms, including, for example, agree to respect others, take responsibility for and accept the consequences of your words, be willing to keep an open mind, dare to engage yourself—comfort is overrated (Samuels, 2009c).

Another way to initiate the discussion of group norms is to ask students to recall their worst experiences in other courses and to think about what rule or norm might have alleviated that situation. Either way, asking students what they need to create an effective community-learning environment is the key to this endeavor. The focus is not necessarily on what makes each individual more willing to participate in the class (because one student might feel very comfortable talking more than their fair share, for example), but rather what would make the learning experience more effective for the community as a whole. A verbal or written commitment from each student ensures buy-in and a willingness to engage with one another respectfully. Incidentally, every class member, including the lead educator, is bound by the community agreement. Thus, everyone is held accountable for their behavior.

Once the class has discussed how to be in the room, it can be useful to consider who is in the room. Ice-breaking activities abound in educational literature. Before choosing one or a few to do in class, it might be useful to consider how this activity will welcome students, get them to know one another better, challenge them to consider their own assumptions and biases, and discover what they may have in common with other classmates. A simple exercise is to go around the room asking everyone to share something about themselves that others may not have guessed. These kinds of activities can be used regardless of the subject matter. Again, because students learn best when they are fully engaged, minimizing the mental noise of stereotypes and other microaggressions clears the path for concentration and collaboration.

TRANSFORMING THE CAMPUS/SCHOOL

Creating and maintaining a multicultural learning environment that respects and welcomes all institution members is a long-term, collaborative, dynamic process. It involves bringing together institution members who represent all aspects of the organization to assess the current cultural climate and set goals for the future (Anti-Defamation League, 2005; Micklos, 2013). Kalev, Dobbin, and Kelly (2006) stress the importance of institutionalized formal diversity practices and policy. Many of these practices over their 30-year longitudinal study were still in place, as opposed to diversity champions who may come and go and whose work may or may not be continued once the individual leaves the organization or moves to a different department.

The multicultural approach stresses the advantages that a diverse organizational membership brings and views social differences as a well of strength (Cox, 1991). Ely and Thomas (2001) suggest that bringing diverse cultural ideals and knowledge into organizational decisionmaking leads to more inclusive, effective, and robust strategies of innovation. Creating a diverse membership, however, has its challenges, one of which is overcoming the condition of code-switching.

Beyond Code-Switching

Code-switching, or "language subordination" (Lippi-Green, 2012), is the notion that members of traditionally marginalized groups must leave their ethnic or cultural identity at the door when they walk into the educational institution and take on an identity of the dominant culture. This is often done as an assimilationist practice that is usually encouraged, if not demanded, most often to make members of the dominant culture feel more comfortable. Unfortunately, this deleterious practice has serious implications for the retention of traditionally marginalized group members (Cox, 1993) in that it calls for the rejection of the communities that define them. After all,

> we do not . . . ask a person to change the color of her skin, her religion, her gender, her sexual identity, but we regularly demand of people that they suppress or deny the most effective way they have of situating themselves socially in the world. (Lippi-Green, 2012, p. 66)

In an inclusive environment, faculty, staff, and students should be allowed to bring their entire identities into the building and/or onto campus.

Support for Educators

Micklos (2013) suggests that building relationships and good communication are important steps to welcoming and retaining organization members of diverse backgrounds. Among his recommendations are developing mentoring programs for members of traditionally marginalized groups and providing professional development to encourage aptitude in cultural responsiveness. He is not the only scholar suggesting multicultural training for educators. In 2013, the Stanford Center for Opportunity Policy in Education (SCOPE) and the National Education Policy Center (NEPC) published a report that provides recommendations for establishing effective culturally inclusive policies in schools to close the opportunity gap. The report includes the training of teachers so that they have a profound understanding not only of cultural differences, but also how inequality impacts them. In addition, the report affirms the importance of integrating culturally relevant curricula in the classroom, and just as important, the promotion of efforts that will change the attitudes and beliefs of teachers, administrators, and students about teaching, learning, and student ability.

Monocultural to Multicultural Schools/Campuses

Interactive phase theory bridges the gap between monocultural and multicultural classrooms (McIntosh, 1990). Gorski (n.d.) expounds on the five-stage process of transformation toward multicultural education for a school or campus. Stage 1 is "Status Quo," where all materials and teaching tools focus on the mainstream voices and experiences of White Christian males. Stage 2 is known as "Heroes and Holidays," where there is an acknowledgment of diversity and even a celebration of social differences, but only at specific times for specific events (Martin Luther King Day, for example). Stage 3 is an "Integration" phase in which the educator makes an effort to incorporate diverse materials into the curriculum, but that material is still perceived only as supplementary to the mainstream White, Christian, male standpoint.

"Structural Reform" is Stage 4, and redefines the framework of teaching to present multicultural perspectives, not as an add-on, but firmly interwoven into the curriculum. Educators in this stage are committed to continuous education about multicultural histories, perspectives, and materials to incorporate into their teaching. Student perspectives are also encouraged and valued in this stage. Still, multicultural programs and initiatives may be somewhat piecemeal or short-lived. In the final stage, "Transformative Multicultural Education," the focus is on the equity of all students. Social justice concepts of systemic oppression (racism, sexism, heterosexism, and so forth) are taught; students are empowered to challenge these systems in the texts and media they consume, as well as on an interpersonal and community level; and social activism is encouraged.

Recruitment and Retention

A recent article in the *Chronicle of Higher Education* asserts the importance of establishing a supportive environment before a new faculty member is even hired. Roy (2013) elucidates:

> We should ask ourselves: What kind of support does the candidate need to succeed here? Can it be put in place before she arrives on campus? These same questions should be asked whether a faculty member is white, brown, or black, gay or straight, is or is not physically challenged, is a woman or a man. The answers will depend on many factors, including a clear-eyed assessment of the prevailing culture in the department and the university as a whole.

Roy also suggests, as other scholars have, that mentoring junior faculty paves the way for retention of members of traditionally marginalized groups, and that mentors should be rewarded for their time, effort, and service through the tenure and promotion process. Further, she acknowledges the challenging role, specifically, that faculty of color face. Their expected contributions to campuses range from serving on search committees to mentoring students of color to championing diversity and inclusiveness issues on campus, all while teaching and doing research. These obligations must be kept to a minimum, especially when a faculty member is working toward tenure.

Active recruitment of educators with traditionally marginalized identities from college, master's, and doctoral programs is another effective inclusiveness initiative. Finally, Roy argues for "cluster hires": Hiring two or more faculty members from traditionally marginalized groups makes it more likely that they will stay at the institution. Often, these faculty members leave in favor of a more diverse community. With critical mass comes a cultural shift of an organization that serves to welcome and retain a diverse membership.

What would an inclusive educational institution look like? One way we know we have reached success is if we can honestly say we have created, as Chrobot Mason (2003) describes it, "a comfortable, non-threatening environment" for all (p. 7). This could be assessed through climate surveys of the entire organization—in other words, not just assessment of students, but also of faculty and administrators. A standard would need to be put in place to determine where the organization stands currently and what the organization ideally expects. The images on the walls in classrooms, offices, and hallways would reflect diverse students, faculty, and staff members. The physical space would have wide hallways and doorways to accommodate anyone who needs more room. The buildings would incorporate gathering areas with chairs and/or sofas to encourage relationship building. The website for the institution would include a link on its homepage to a well-managed diversity and inclusiveness page. Signs around the building or campus would advertise the many multicultural activities going on. And the list goes on. In the following chapter, we will consider the factors that challenge inclusiveness and some of the strategies educators can use to build multicultural environments and relationships.

CHAPTER 5

Going Deeper: Reflecting on What We Don't Know We Don't Know

> In order to become a multicultural teacher you must first be a multicultural person.
>
> —*Sonia Nieto*

A colleague/friend, Simon, practices multicultural inclusiveness as a clinical counselor. As a White male, he has studied what makes a multicultural environment and implemented these practices. He has created office space that is warm and welcoming; he made sure that his office was physically accessible to clients and their family members; he only takes health insurance from companies that support women's and LGBTQ communities' needs; he doesn't put up a Christmas tree in the lobby in December to ensure that all of his clients, regardless of their religious/spiritual practices, feel respected; and he spends his own time learning all he can about cultures that are different from his own. One day, he welcomed a young Latina client into his office. He began his usual intake process, but when it came to discussing why she was there, he noticed that she became nervous. She admitted that she was undocumented in the United States and that that was causing her some anxiety. Wanting to make her feel as comfortable as possible, Simon did not flinch at this disclosure; rather, he went right on with his questions about what else might be causing her tension. Among other things, she mentioned her immigrant status three different times during their session. Still, my colleague did not engage her on the topic.

It wasn't until after the client left that Simon reviewed the situation in his mind. What he realized was that although his goal was to make the client feel welcomed and included by not reacting to her immigrant status, he ended up missing out on an important piece of why she had come to him in the first place. His antiracist intentions skewed their session to the point that his own practiced counseling skills were rendered almost useless.

Simon was baffled by his own behavior, but in the context of multicultural preparedness, his actions make sense. He was taught to be respectful of social differences, and in a way, he was, but he, like all of us in society, was also taught that talking about differences could target him as being exclusionary at best and racist at worst. So he chose to skip over the entire conversation in an effort to be inclusive. What he began to realize when he reflected on his actions was, first, that it takes a lot of self-reflection to behave inclusively, and second, that there are different levels of multicultural awareness and behavior, and he needed to know more.

Simon's situation demonstrates that *practicing inclusiveness* means not only checking off the boxes of inclusive practices, but also reflecting deeply on one's own identities, biases, and behaviors. It means acknowledging that we are going to make mistakes, which we can offer ourselves grace for, and which we hope will become valuable lessons for the future. It means learning all we can about cultures that are different from our own, and then meeting someone from that culture and not making assumptions based on that knowledge. It means acquiring a working familiarity of social differences and then putting that aside to relate, authentically, to another human being. I am not advocating colorblindness or identity-blindness—I am suggesting acknowledging, accepting, even embracing differences, while at the same time understanding that people are more than their differences; they are living beings.

TRANSFORMING OUR SELVES

Transformation begins with deep self-reflection. And it invites us to consider what we don't know we don't know, so that we are prepared to teach to a variety of student identities. If we are under the misconception that identity-blindness is a positive goal to shoot for, consider the LGBTQ students in our classrooms who do not see themselves reflected in the course materials. Consider the assumptions that we might make and, in spite of our best intentions, the microaggressions that we might be perpetuating. Identities affect us all. They are not separate from our educational experience. They are inexorably intertwined and can create either an environment of inclusion for students, or a barrier to learning.

Because most teachers have not been given an opportunity for self-reflection, they may not know if something they say or do might be construed as offensive to others. Sue et al. (2007) confirmed this need by stating, "The prerequisite for cultural competence has always been . . . self-awareness" (p. 283). Training for all educational professionals must include the subtle forms of racism, sexism, heterosexism, and so on that they might perpetuate unknowingly. For example, Sadker and Sadker's (1995) well-known research demonstrates what teachers don't know they don't know. Going into schools with video cameras, the researchers openly divulged that they were studying gender equity. Many teachers eagerly volunteered to be videotaped, believing that their classrooms were exemplars of gender equity. After their classroom behavior was videotaped, the teachers were allowed to review the tape. Even when they watched themselves on camera, they did not see any discrepancy between the way they had treated the boys and the way they had treated girls in class.

Sadker and Sadker, however, found that boys are given more time to answer questions than girls, well-behaved girls get much less attention from teachers as compared with boys, gender segregation abounds, and teachers are more likely to comment on how *smart* a boy is and how *pretty* a girl is. It wasn't until these specific instances of gender inequity were pointed out to the teachers that they finally understood that they weren't as equitable as they had thought. The researchers concluded, "It is difficult to detect sexism unless you know precisely how to observe" (p. 4). And they added, "If a lifetime of socialization makes it difficult to spot gender bias even when you're looking for it, how much harder it is to avoid the traps when you are the one doing the teaching" (p. 4). Learning how to critique our own attitudes and behavior with a social justice lens is the first step in creating inclusive classrooms.

STEREOTYPES AND CONFIRMATION BIAS

As has been iterated throughout this book, education on social justice issues necessitates considering one's own attitudes and how those biases might influence others, even unintentionally. As troubling as it is to admit, a substantial body of evidence confirms that the ways we perceive people and treat them is significantly correlated with the stereotypes we hold to be true, even in spite of our best intentions (Kunda, 1999; Lepore & Brown, 1997; Powell, 2012; Stangor, 2001; Van Ryn & Fu, 2003). Worse still, the psychological theory known as confirmation bias asserts that when we perceive someone's behavior as challenging a stereotype we expect, rather than rethinking our ingrained assumptions, we are more likely to either ignore the behavior or consider the behavior anomalous—the exception to the rule (Blasi, 2001; Darley & Gross, 1983). Powell (2012) suggests that because these thought processes often occur at a subconscious level, they are not easily overcome.

The good news, however, is that it is, in fact, possible to challenge those automatic, unconscious, reductive stereotypes so that we can begin to treat people as the complex individuals that they are. Van Ryn and Fu (2003) suggests three ways we can do this. First, we must be willing to accept that we do, in fact, have biases, and make ourselves aware of them. Second, we must be determined not only to unearth our own stereotypes, but also to challenge them. And finally, we need to learn how to exchange those automatic biases for different, more inclusive, notions.

EIGHT TRANSFORMATIVE STEPS TO BUILDING CULTURAL INCLUSIVENESS

In order to navigate this challenging path, I offer an eight-step transformative process that can be used to build authentic multicultural inclusiveness. The steps include (1) Discovering Our Own Biases, (2) Reflecting on Our (Systemic) Socialization, (3) Challenging Our Assumptions, (4) Reflecting on Our Own Identities, (5) Contemplating Our Emotions, (6) Reflecting on Our Behavior, (7) Considering Our Purpose, and (8) Committing to This Work. Each step proposes specific questions that we can ask ourselves along the way.

Step 1: Discovering Our Own Biases

We can ask ourselves: What are the messages we have learned about women, gay people, lesbians, people in poverty, Latinos, people with disabilities, older people, Black people, large people, Muslims, and so forth? We need to be aware of our implicit biases, making the invisible visible to ourselves. In other words, we must acknowledge that we have learned misinformation about many different groups, even our own, and then shed light on those misperceptions. Without that explicit self-reflection, we don't know the extent of the challenge before us. We can tell ourselves and everyone else that "we don't have a prejudiced bone in our body," but the reality is that cultural stereotypes abound, and unfortunately, just by living in the culture, through osmosis, our perceptions about ourselves and others become severely impacted.

The Implicit Association Test can help with this, as outlined in Chapter 1, and/or we can make a list of our own learned biases; either process can be eye-opening. I recommend making a list on your own rather than in a group or workshop. Many negative consequences can arise from doing this particular kind of work in a group, including reifying stereotypes, which is the antithesis of the goal of this exercise. In addition, in a group, this activity may not be effective based on Social Desirability Theory: Most people don't want to admit that they have biases against particular groups, let alone share that information with others. You may choose to shred the evidence once the list has been created, but making the list is the important part.

Step 2: Reflecting on Our (Systemic) Socialization

Once we are more aware of the negative stereotypes we hold, we can ask: How do we know what we know? Where did the damaging myths we have bought into come from? Which institutions have misinformed us? What kinds of experiences have we had that have contributed to our assumptions about other people? Pinpointing the starting place (family, school, media, and so on) of our learned behavior can give us insight into the propaganda to which we have been exposed. Our attitudes are formed at least in part by social institutions. It is not necessarily a causal relationship, but rather a mutually perpetuating one because institutions are made up of individuals. Since these foundations exist in a society that perpetuates inequality, they not only tend to discriminate internally, but also maintain and spread the notions. This, in turn, has dire consequences for our individual attitudes, and often for our behavior.

For example, our culture teaches us primarily through the media that Black men are dangerous, out of control, and should be feared. Consider how that single assumption might impact the way educators treat Black students. Will they be less likely to trust Black students? Will they be more likely to expect negative or even disruptive behavior from Black students? In fact, many studies have shown that students of color are much more likely to receive significantly harsher disciplinary action, expulsion, and suspension than White students for the same or similar problem behavior, based primarily on implicit assumptions that we have learned (Skiba et al., 2011; Wallace, Goodkind, Wallace, & Bachman, 2008). Figuring out where these ideas come from helps us understand how stereotypes are socially constructed and perpetuated, and reminds us that they can be unlearned.

In the same vein, it is useful to consider our past experiences and how they might have affected our attitudes about people who are different from us. Sometimes, we make assumptions about a whole group of people based on our experiences with a single member of a particular group. Many years ago, while traveling in Israel, I was chatting with an Israeli soldier at a café. I was stunned by the invective he spewed against Palestinians. As our conversation proceeded, I was able to ask the soldier about his past. After a time, he happened to mention that when he was a young boy, he had witnessed a Palestinian man stabbing his (the soldier's) father to death. It was clear to me that this experience, aside from the horrific trauma and loss of his father, had had a profound impact on him, molding his attitudes and behaviors. As we talked, I mentioned that this evil act he had witnessed did not represent the actions of all Palestinians, but only those of one man. Making this leap to break away from stereotyping is, for some people, an insurmountable challenge, but it has the potential to bring peace to someone with a grief-stricken heart. Without understanding our own or others' past experiences with members of other cultures, it is difficult to fully comprehend the extent to which we adhere to our preconceived notions. Learning what these experiences are can help us understand more about our own or others' belief systems, and can pave the way for letting go of these stereotypes.

Step 3: Challenging Our Assumptions

Once we are more cognizant of where our biases came from, they become easier to confront. Best-selling author Byron Katie's (2002) work revolves around the notion of challenging our thoughts and thought processes. She proposes Four Questions we can ask to lead us through that process, which (with some minor modifications that I have taken the liberty of making) can be applied to stereotypes. Katie's first question is: Is it true? The assumptions we make about ourselves and others may or may not be true. Regardless, we put a lot of energy into maintaining our thoughts and beliefs without considering their veracity. Moreover, if we blindly consider stereotypes to be true, we deny the person about whom we are making assumptions the opportunity to defy our biases, getting stuck in confirmation bias.

The second question is: Can we absolutely know that it is true? This question applies especially if the answer to the first question was yes. Either way, it calls into question how we came to know these "truths," and whether they are, in actuality, just assumptions. It also reminds us that even if the idea is sometimes true or is true for one person based on our past experience, nothing is true for every single person in any socially constructed category.

The third question takes the thought process a bit deeper by asking: What happens when we believe that idea? This question asks us to consider the consequences of believing what we believe. How does this "truth"/assumption affect us? Our emotions? How do those emotions manifest in our body and affect our behavior? How does this "truth" affect our relationships? How does it affect the way we interact both with people we know and those we are just meeting?

Finally, the fourth question is: What would our life/thoughts/actions be like without the idea we are considering? This last question can be incredibly transformative and freeing. It asks us to consider how our lives and interactions would be affected if we were to let go of our assumptions, liberating us from long-held misconceptions. This freedom from restrictive mythical notions allows us to treat others as individuals.

For some folks, it might be useful to add a fifth question to the list. It is not always necessary, but in some situations, it can help us move forward if we are stuck. My addendum to Katie's Four Questions would be: What might be a truth that supersedes the myth you just debunked? In other words, in certain circumstances, it is helpful to acknowledge that what you thought was truth was merely an assumption that you were taught. Now that you are aware that it is only an assumption, what might a different truth be? For example, if you had a notion about a certain group of people, and through this process you realized that the idea was only a stereotype, what might you teach yourself instead? Perhaps it could be something along the lines of "Each individual has the potential to behave in a positive way or a negative way, regardless of their social identities." Or, "One person can never represent a whole social group." Or it could be something more positive, such as "Every person ultimately seeks peace and well-being."

Research shows that when we challenge a stereotype in our minds before we interact with someone who is a member of a particular social group, we can overcome our biases. Powell (2012) cites three ways that science has shown we can conquer negative biases. The first is by viewing *positive* images of people from stereotyped groups. Even simply invoking those images in our minds can overcome bias. Second, when organization members see a person of color in a leadership position, prejudice decreases throughout the organization. And third, cross-cultural relationships reduce implicit bias. Powell's findings inform these transformational steps.

Step 4: Reflecting on Our Own Identities

We can ask: How do our own social identities (race, gender, sexuality, age, disability, and so on) affect our assumptions about ourselves and others? How do our social identities affect the way we interact with people who have different social identities than we do? Stereotypes run deep, and can affect even our own perceptions of ourselves. The sociological term for this concept is *internalized oppression*, or conversely, *internalized privilege* (Samuels, 2009a). Internalized oppression occurs when people who are disadvantaged in society based on a particular social group membership believe as true the stereotypes and attitudes that are directed at their group. This can create a self-loathing that we may not even be aware of because it seeps in subconsciously from the negative messages to which we are exposed daily in our culture.

One example of this is media bias. The media are more likely to portray people of color as lawbreakers and White people as law defenders (Dixon & Linz, 2000). This leads to the increased likelihood that women will clutch their purses close to them in the presence of an African American man (Oliver, 2003). As an educator, my biggest concern is how this affects Black students. How would it feel to constantly be considered a threat? What is the psychological impact of that notion? How does that stereotype squash a Black male student's humanity, and what are the consequences to his self-esteem and efficacy to succeed? Moreover, how does internalized oppression manifest when the media spend a disproportionate amount of time emphasizing the school-to-prison pipeline rather than the nearly half a million African American students in college, which is quadruple the number of African American men in prison (Fenwick, 2013)?

The flip side of the coin is internalized privilege, which occurs when people are advantaged/given the benefit of the doubt based on a particular social group membership, and when they believe that the stereotypes and attitudes that are directed at their group are true. Internalized privilege breeds entitlement. In the example above, the fact that White people are more often portrayed as defenders of the law has an impact on us all. It signals to everyone, and especially to White people, that White people can be trusted. Thus, when a White person breaks the law, it is not at all uncommon for them to claim that it was a person of color who actually committed the crime. Often, the White criminals are believed (Russell-Brown, 1998).

Internalized privilege also includes an element of invisibility. Those who are privileged in a certain category are the standard against which everyone else is measured and named, and therefore they don't typically see their status as privileged, but rather as the norm. For example, even though we live in a heteronormative society, where the assumption and the expectation is that everyone is heterosexual, when we think or hear someone discussing sexuality, *homosexuality* is what comes to mind. In fact, heterosexuals are not typically cognizant of even having a sexual orientation, and they do not need to worry about stereotype threat based on their sexuality. That freedom from anxiety is an invisible privilege that most LGBTQ people do not get.

Oppression and privilege are intertwined with exclusion and inclusion; thus, it is important in this process to consider: How do institutionalized systems of inequality affect *me*? Which of my own social identities *allow* me access to benefits that are denied to others? Which of my own social identities *deny* me access to resources that are provided to others based on social group membership? How do these inequalities play out in my own daily life? How have I been socialized to think about others, based on their social group memberships? How do I treat people differently based on those memberships? Answering these questions honestly, in spite of the discomfort they may bring up, is vital in this transformative process.

If we are unaware of the unearned advantages and disadvantages that are bestowed upon us by our socially constructed society, we may be missing the systemic ways privilege and oppression operate in our own lives.

Based on our social identities, we are taught whom to trust, whom to avoid, whom to idolize, and whom to demonize. For example, do we see police officers as allies who will protect us and keep us safe, or as systemic profilers whom we must hide from to keep *ourselves* safe? Our work is to figure out how our own social identities have contributed to our ideas about ourselves and others, and how we might unintentionally be perpetuating systemic inequities at the individual level by being inclusive of some people at the expense of others.

Step 5: Contemplating Our Emotions

We can ask: Which emotions arise when we think about people who have different social identities from ours? What feelings come up when we think about people in poverty? People with disabilities? Transgender individuals? Older people? These questions are certainly socially constructed in that how we are taught to feel about various groups is based on the culture in which we live. For example, in some cultures, aged individuals are considered wise and treated with the utmost respect, even revered. In other cultures, such as mainstream U.S. society, senior citizens are considered out of touch with current events, contemporary language, and present-day ideas, and so the emotion that might arise when we see them is one of disdain or annoyance. Once again, it is important to acknowledge the emotions we have toward others. Do we feel an underlying fear or foreboding around people with disabilities? Do we feel a sense of pity around people in poverty? Do we feel a sense of confusion around transgender people?

Unfortunately, as mentioned, our unchallenged biases and assumptions about others serve to separate us from one another. Further, separation and fear are mutually perpetuating: The more we segregate ourselves from one another, the more misunderstandings occur, and the more assumptions increase and fear arises. When we are afraid, we tend to withdraw even more, and not only do we miss the opportunity to challenge our assumptions, but also we tend to exclude members of that group even more, in favor of the comfort of being around people who look like we do.

On the other hand, if we are aware that we have negative feelings toward members of a specific group, then we can compassionately consider those feelings when they arise. We can even forgive ourselves for the misinformation we have systematically received, and go through the process of letting go of those negative feelings. Connecting with others in a genuine way can lead us away from discomfort and anxiety to warm feelings and inclusive attitudes and behaviors.

We must contemplate the feelings we have about others before we can truly connect with them. The goal is not to deny or stifle these feelings, but to acknowledge them and let them go. If we ignore that those feelings exist, we run the risk of allowing those emotions to gain control over both our attitudes and behaviors, which can cause us to discriminate unconsciously. Acknowledging those feelings, in contrast, gives us a choice about how we behave, and as a result, we are more likely to act inclusively. These ideas have led me to consider the possibility that in my research study outlined in Chapter 2, it may be that the participants had never been given the opportunity to reflect on their emotions and attitudes. Without deep self-reflection, they may have simply assumed that they behave inclusively, despite the fact that their behaviors tended to paint a slightly different picture. Perhaps if they had considered their own emotions and biases, preparing themselves to interact cross-culturally, they might have realized that it is the implicit assumptions and emotions that, despite our best intentions, can contribute to our exclusion of others.

Step 6: Reflecting on Our Own Behavior

We can ask: How have our false beliefs, assumptions, and stereotypes operated in our daily lives and/or in the classroom? The research by Skiba et al. (2011) mentioned in Step 2 above is a prime example of how our biases can lead to the excessive discipline of Black students. These research findings demonstrate the depth of these preconceived notions, because it is likely that few, if any, of the teachers who were recommending expulsion or suspension for Black students would do so knowing that they were acting on stereotypes. It is also unlikely that they would consider themselves racist in any way. The disconnect here is between our unknown biases and our resulting actions.

This is where microaggressions and stereotype threat seep into our classrooms. Without even knowing it, we might be creating a "hostile" environment, one in which some students are feeling excluded. One example of this is making the assumption that all students have access to the Internet in their homes. Although we might be aware that not all students have the means to afford their own computer, much less a monthly Internet connection, we still might slip and say, "Just Google it for homework." The underlying message is that everyone is, at minimum, lower-middle-class. The impact, regardless of the benign intention, could be anguish for a student in poverty. The goal is not to be cautious with every word that comes out of our mouths, but rather to be mindful of our cultural differences.

As we consider our behavior, situating ourselves in Hardiman and Jackson's (1997) Social Identity Development model outlined in Chapter 1 can serve several purposes. First, it gives us an idea of how far we have come along the spectrum of multicultural inclusiveness. Second, it allows us to consider how the stage of development we are in affects both our attitudes and our behavior toward others. Third, it can provide insight into where and why we might be stuck in a certain stage. And finally, it offers direction and a goal to strive for in terms of becoming the best multicultural advocate possible.

Step 7: Considering Our Purpose

We can ask: How do racism, sexism, heterosexism, ageism, disability, religious intolerance, and so on personally hurt me? How would I benefit if they no longer existed? It took me a very long time to understand the impact of these atrocities that we continue to tolerate in our society. As a Jewish person, I was keenly aware of how religious intolerance can devalue a person's beliefs and make a person feel excluded. As a woman, I knew that fighting for women's equality was incredibly important. As a White person, however, it was unclear to me how racism was hurting me, personally. I was aware of the damage it was doing to people of color, and I knew the responsibility was mine to be an antiracist advocate, but how was it affecting me?

It finally became clear to me over the course of my first few years of attending the annual award-winning White Privilege Conference (WPC). The WPC is an intersectional, interdisciplinary conference that founder Dr. Eddie Moore, Jr. describes as way beyond Diversity 101. It takes into account all systems of oppression and privilege (not just race) and challenges participants to consciously and deeply reflect, engage, learn, and connect cross-culturally. My experience at the conference quickly went from participant to member of the national planning team. I knew I had found the community I wanted and needed to be a part of.

My experience with the WPC has not been without its challenges, and I have learned so much in this and other radically multicultural environments. One big lesson for me has been to discover just how much racism has negatively affected me personally. I have learned that racism causes separation between people and, sometimes, distrust. I have learned that preconceived notions about me as a White person have sometimes led people of color (accurately or inaccurately) to treat me as an opponent rather than a friend. I have learned that my skin color means something; it represents something, whether I want it to or not. I know there are times when I, even unintentionally, misuse my privilege by, for example, taking up more than my fair share of space (verbally or physically). When I become aware of my easily manifested entitlement, I tangibly feel the sting of inequality, even as the recipient of unearned privilege. It is important that I have deeply felt this pain, not as White guilt, but as a reminder that these systems of inequality affect us all, obviously to different degrees, and that my objective is to dismantle them.

Another personal example that reminds me why I must remain committed to this work happened recently at another social justice conference. A participant and I were the only White people in the room. I was very aware that the other White participant seemed to be "showing her White privilege" in terms of trying to direct the conversation a certain way, focusing on the outcome rather than the process, and in general, being what I perceived as overbearing. Her nervous energy was palpable.

As I witnessed this, I grew more and more uncomfortable. I was wracking my brain trying not to judge the White woman, and at the same time trying to figure out how to politely and gently challenge the Whiteness in the room, but I couldn't come up with a compassionate way to do so. So, rather than challenging it head-on, I chose to try to distance myself from her. I tried to engage the group in a gentler way, wanting to connect instead with the positive energy in the room.

Apparently, I was not successful. What I received was a noticeable distancing of the people of color in the room from me; they were not engaging with me. These were folks I knew fairly well and I was taken aback by their reaction. I became so uncomfortable both from the Whiteness and the reaction to it that I chose to quietly get up and leave the room so that I could process what was happening. I didn't want to create more drama, but I knew I couldn't remain in that space any longer.

While outside, I searched my own feelings and realized that deep down, I was incredibly hurt that I was being lumped together with the Whiteness in the room. I felt dishonored and unappreciated. And at the same time, I felt the shame of what Whiteness has come to mean. And in that moment I realized that this is, in fact, the by-product of White supremacy. It became clear to me that I needed to practice what I teach. I needed to accept that White privilege causes chasms between people, and that my job as a White ally is to acknowledge and to try to understand the tension that my White skin can cause, regardless of my own words or actions.

I also remembered that I often advise others that this social justice journey is a marathon, not a sprint. White supremacy has permeated our culture so deeply that I must be patient when trying to dismantle it. I then remembered that I have the privilege of being able to leave the room when necessary. And that's when it occurred to me that I must go back. I remembered that my job is to show up for the relationship, and to keep showing up. Building relationships includes building trust and showing that you are someone other people can count on not to shy away from the work. I also did not want to let the inevitable mistakes that come from building relationships across difference hold me back.

It is my job as an antiracist activist to confront the Whiteness in the room when I see it. When I think back on the incident, I can see that leaving the scenario was one way of disrupting the status quo. It demonstrated resistance to what was happening. Could I have done things differently, and better? Absolutely! I could have been more transparent with my protest. But either way, what I received when I returned to the room showed me that these ways of creating change can make a difference. The energy in the room had changed; the other White participant was no longer taking over, and I was honored with an incredibly supportive welcome from my friends of color in the room. I know there are many ways to disrupt White supremacy. Both verbal and nonverbal challenges are called for. This experience made it clear to me that this is powerful work. It showed me that White supremacy can be dismantled, slowly, relationship by relationship. It is a lifelong commitment and a practice that takes patience and faith, and I know I am not alone when I say it is well worth the effort (Samuels, 2013a).

Recognizing how systems of inequality affect us personally helps us consider how we might personally benefit from dedicating ourselves to social justice ideals and practices. For if we are only doing this work in service to members of traditionally marginalized groups, what happens when it gets difficult? What happens when we make a mistake? How likely will we be to throw in the towel and say, "Well, I tried"? The more we can identify the specific ways in which doing this work benefits us at a personal level, the more likely we will be to stick with it for the long haul. This is an opportunity to ask ourselves what kind of world we want to live in. I know I am creating that world every single time I stand up against injustice, especially when I do so with compassion. Creating the world I want to live in, for me, is a lofty goal and a worthwhile purpose.

Step 8: Committing to This Work

We can ask: For how long are we willing to commit to learning about diversity and building inclusiveness? About which social identities do we know the least? Where are our *blind spots* (Banaji & Greenwald, 2013), and what kind of effort are we willing to make to continue our training? In the course of our education, we might have learned or taught ourselves important information about some social identities, but missed out on learning about others. Although we can never know everything about every social group, the alternative is not necessarily to learn nothing about anyone. We can commit to learning about specific cultures by learning a new language, or listening to a radio station aimed at a culture that is different from our own. We can make an effort to attend multicultural events in our communities or go to meetings and get educated on the issues a particular culture faces at the local, regional, and/or global level.

This process also entails a certain amount of perspective taking. It is crucial that educators and administrators, in particular, go out of our way to understand the viewpoints and experiences of other campus members, especially students. Otherwise, problems can arise when "educators think they know about the lived experience of others; are in a position to speak on behalf of others' experiences; and do so through solely their own identities, experiences, and lens of privilege" (Arminio, Torres, & Pope, 2012, p. 187). In reality, we all have limited perspectives. Broadening those perspectives is fundamental to building inclusiveness, for this work cannot be done successfully in a vacuum.

When I began my own process of social justice work, I thought if I learned enough about other cultures (as though there is such a thing!), worked at it long enough, and challenged myself enough, I would suddenly become unbiased about all different social groups. I thought that perhaps one day I would wake up and no longer have preconceived notions about others. Many years later, that still has not happened, and I've come to the conclusion that it never will. Because I am constantly bombarded with racist, sexist, heterosexist, ageist, and other biased messages through the culture, the media, the education system, and so forth, I do my best to challenge these notions. However, simply being part of the system of inequalities, as Johnson (2006) explains, means that we cannot escape these biased thoughts.

The good news is that the more we challenge these offensive ideas when they come up in our own minds, the more obvious they become everywhere else—in the media, in our culture, in our classrooms—and the more we can put forth our efforts into changing these ideas. Unlearning misinformation, however, is a lifelong endeavor. The goal is not to figure out our preconceived notions and then blame ourselves for being bad people. Instead, the idea is to accept that there are stereotypes we have believed, acknowledge where they came from, and with compassion, challenge ourselves every single time we notice them. We can reframe our assumptions with counter-stereotypes. This is how we can create change. The process does take time and effort, but it can be incredibly rewarding. The suggested eight steps lead us to the ultimate goal of being able to develop relationships across difference, which is the key to building inclusiveness.

CHAPTER 6

Building Inclusiveness Across Difference

> I think we have to own the fears that we have of each other, and then, in some practical way, some daily way, figure out how to see people differently than the way we were brought up to.
>
> —*Alice Walker*

Building relationships means that we will make mistakes. Rather than allowing those mistakes to deter us from intercultural connections, we can let our mistakes serve as stepping-stones to developing inclusiveness. When I hear the phrase "We learn from our mistakes," I have always thought that the unspoken end to the sentence was ". . . so we won't make the same mistake twice." The underlying message to me was always that making mistakes is the worst thing we can do, and that we should spend our lives doing everything in our power to avoid them.

Over time, I've come to realize, first, that if we go through life trying to avoid any specific thing, we're not really living. Second, if we believe that making mistakes is something we should feel shame and embarrassment about, then when we err, we begin to perceive ourselves as bad people, undeserving of compassion. In turn, the process of shame and blame feels so bad that we do everything in our power not to feel that way again by living in fear of making mistakes. And the cycle continues.

Instead of getting lost in the guilt and shame we feel, we can ask ourselves: What did I just learn that I didn't know before? If we look deeper than "I learned that I should never say or do that again," we can usually pinpoint some way that a long-held belief or stereotype was challenged. For example, when a friend was transitioning from Female to Male, I knew intellectually that his Preferred Gender Pronoun (PGP) was *he/him*. Unfortunately, what came out of my mouth sometimes was *she* or *her*. My intention was to support him completely. I could even tell myself that my mistakes were made simply because I had known him for many years as a woman. And he was so gracious when I got it wrong, I hope, because he understood that my underlying goal was to support him in any way I could.

Yet I knew that this was a microaggression that had dire consequences, as they all do. So guilt and shame ensued. When I looked deeper, I was able to come to terms with the depth of my learned transphobia. I could focus on where I held my fear and discomfort in my body, and let them go. Being transphobic is not the way I want to live my life. We can use our mistakes as stepping-stones in our social justice journeys.

As Roy (2013) recommends, "We're going to have to ask each other for forgiveness ahead of time for the many mistakes we will make as we try to communicate cross-culturally" (para. 13). Our lives and realities are based on our perceptions. Therefore, we have an opportunity to perceive things differently from how we are used to. By their very nature, mistakes are not made on purpose; it is usually only afterward when we perceive our comment or behavior as a mistake that we start to believe that it actually was a mistake. What if we choose to view mistakes differently—even, perhaps, as inevitable? They can be reframed as opportunities to learn something about ourselves that we didn't know before. The goal is to learn to be our authentic selves with everyone with whom we engage.

Without going through the deep process of self-reflection, it is unlikely that we will be truly successful in cross-cultural relationships. Learning the truth about the lived experiences of people who have different identities from ours is only possible through relationship building. Sure, we can educate ourselves on these issues, but the value comes from using what we've learned to create bonds with others.

TRANSFORMING OUR RELATIONSHIPS

In academic settings, or really in any setting, a sense of social connectedness, belonging, and social support correlates with many positive outcomes (Walton & Cohen, 2007). For students, belongingness increases academic achievement and persistence in school (Mahoney & Cairns, 1997; Ryan & Deci, 2000); that is, when students feel safe and welcomed, they can focus their thoughts and energy on learning (Anti-Defamation League, 2005). For all of us, belongingness decreases our chances of both mental and physical health problems (Bolger, Zuckerman, & Kessler, 2000), among other positive consequences. Positive interactions tend to lead to diminished fear of others, paving the way for wholeheartedness, creativity, and innovation to blossom. Thus, regardless of the subjects we teach, taking time to increase collegiality with students, faculty, and staff translates not only to positive outcomes for us, but also leads to a more enthusiastic, healthy campus climate for everyone.

When we have gone through the process of self-reflection, challenged our assumptions, and made a commitment to long-term learning and culturally inclusive practices, building cross-cultural relationships becomes possible. These relationships are not always easy, mostly due to the legacy of historical, institutional inequities. Our society, and our educational system in particular, is not designed to be integrative. Because of all the stereotypes that are continually perpetuated, we are taught to distrust one another. Distrust leads to fear and isolation rather than connection.

The first criterion for building relationships is building trust. Unfortunately, trust develops slowly, and it takes work. Best-selling author and shame researcher Dr. Brené Brown (2012) found that trust requires vulnerability. Unfortunately, our culture trains us to believe that vulnerability is a sign of weakness, but Brown explains,

> To believe vulnerability is weakness is to believe that feeling is weakness. To foreclose on our emotional life out of a fear that the costs will be too high is to walk away from the very thing that gives purpose and meaning to living. . . . Vulnerability is the birthplace of love, belonging, joy, courage, empathy, and creativity. It is the source of hope, empathy, accountability, and authenticity. (pp. 33–34)

In relationship building, being vulnerable does not mean oversharing, but rather "sharing our feelings and our experiences with people who have earned the right to hear them. Being vulnerable and open is mutual and an integral part of the trust-building process" (Brown, 2012, p. 45). The process means taking a risk and being willing to make mistakes. It means recognizing our fears, remembering that our preconceived notions are simply learned, and knowing we have the opportunity to challenge those notions by breaking down the barriers of separation.

To challenge our stereotypes, Sue, Arredondo, and McDavis (1992) suggest becoming actively engaged with members of traditionally marginalized groups outside of the work environment. This allows for a broader perspective of differences and a deeper understanding of needs and experiences—much more than could be realized in a limited academic environment. Unfortunately, racial segregation in the United States abounds, even in terms of friendships. A 2013 Reuters poll found that many Americans have no friends who identify as a different race from them. About 40% of White Americans reported only having White friends, and approximately 25% of people of color have friends only of their own race (Dunsmuir, 2013). Because cross-cultural friendships help reduce bias (Aberson, Shoemaker, & Tomolillo, 2004; Paluck, 2006; Pettigrew & Tropp, 2006), it is imperative that we work toward change in this arena.

Moreover, mistakes and misunderstandings, the inevitable consequences of these relationships, can be overcome by consistency and trust. When (not if) mistakes are made, stereotypes are unintentionally cued, and if the relationship is not strong enough to handle the situation, the connection will likely dissolve. On the other hand, if the relationship is strong, the mistake can be discussed, the friends can learn from it, and ultimately, the connection can be maintained. We are not always aware when we make a mistake, so part of building relationships is to be able to count on our friend to call us out when we do. After all, we cannot learn what we don't know we don't know in isolation. We must build our relationships so that we can make connections across differences a daily, and lifelong, practice.

For example, I was recently spending time with a friend of color when I overzealously responded to an idea he had by saying, "That's *so* smart!" After I said it, I immediately reflected on how my strong reaction could have been taken as surprise that he was capable of such an idea. Although I knew that was not my intention, I challenged myself to consider first, "Would I have had the exact same reaction if he were White?" As my answer was affirmative, I was able to acknowledge that my intention, at least, was not to commit a microaggression. Had I stopped there, however, I would have fallen into the trap of thinking that intent is the only aspect of the comment, behavior, or situation that matters. As Sue (2010) reminds us, impact is critically important to consider when dealing with microaggressions. I checked in with my friend to see how he had taken my response. I was grateful that he trusted that my intention was authentic: that I was genuinely thrilled with his notion. He reminded me that authenticity is what he looks for in a friend, and how he knows he can build trust with that friend over time.

As we strategize about how to challenge those stereotypes, we can heed the guidance Pat Parker (2009) provides in the poem "For the White Person Who Wants to Know How to Be My Friend." Parker writes, "The first thing you do is to forget that i'm Black; Second, you must never forget that i'm Black" (p. 522). I would argue that this lesson could be applied to any social identity. In other words, Parker is suggesting: be aware of my social identities, have some knowledge about them, and then treat me as a human being rather than as the sum total of my differences. This goes beyond political correctness. It is a commitment to genuinely creating authentic, respectful relationships across difference.

This kind of relationship building is critically important in a multicultural classroom. At the 2014 Cherry Creek Diversity Conference, I spoke with an educator in the public school system, Quincy "Q" Shannon. He works with high school students who are labeled *nonmotivated* or *troublemakers*. He has found that the best way to initiate change with these students is to listen. What he has learned is that most of the time, these students have no one in their lives to whom they can tell their stories, hopes, and dreams. Building relationships with these students helps them see themselves as capable (Q. Shannon, personal communication, February 1, 2013), and, I would argue, can make a difference in the lives of students who have been told that they are not.

TRANSFORMING OUR INTERACTIONS

The process of building relationships, however, can get tricky. Often, when we meet someone, especially for the first time, our minds become so muddled with thoughts and our bodies become overwhelmed with the emotions that are surfacing about the experience that it drowns out what the other person is saying. (This is one reason that some people have difficulty remembering the name of a person to whom they were *just* introduced.) When we meet someone, if we are self-conscious about our own thoughts or are desperately trying to challenge our preconceived notions (especially when we are interacting with people who have different social identities from ours), it can seem as if we are being detached, or worse, disingenuous. In this situation, it can be extremely useful to employ the ancient Buddhist practice known as *mindfulness*.

Kabat-Zinn (2013) defines *mindfulness* as awareness of the present moment. Mindfulness means letting go of the "clutter" in our minds, and consciously paying attention, without judgment, to what is occurring right now. It is the notion that we can choose to enter a meeting with another person clouded by assumptions, beliefs, and stereotypes about that person or the meeting itself, or we can be fully present with the person, offering a positive, curious attention simply by choosing to do so.

Many practitioners of mindfulness begin by focusing on their breath. By simply taking a deep breath in and then exhaling, letting go of the clutter, and focusing on the present, mindfulness allows us to interact, to actively listen, and to engage with another person. Rather than spending precious cognitive energy making judgments or challenging our judgments about the person with whom we are speaking, those stereotypes recede into the background as we wholeheartedly engage, paying close attention to what the person before us is saying. With an "empty"/clear head, we may be less likely to stereotype, judge, or make assumptions about not only the person with whom we are speaking but also the person/people/subject about which that person is speaking.

Mindfulness can be utilized in any interpersonal situation, but when it is brought into the classroom, it can have a transformative effect on students and colleagues, alike. As Carter and Wilson's (1994) research on persistence of students of color found, the single most important factor affecting student retention is the quality of interaction they experience with faculty members. Based on the fact that classroom interactions between faculty and students tend to favor students with dominant identities, to whom faculty members give more comprehensive answers and of whom they ask more challenging questions, it is imperative that we work to make all our interactions count.

TRANSFORMING OUR REACTIONS

How do we react when a student, colleague, or supervisor makes an insensitive comment, such as the ones described at the beginning of Chapter 1? Ignoring offensive comments efficiently signals to anyone within hearing distance that the facilitator of the classroom is not an ally to members of traditionally marginalized groups. Although it takes precious class time away from the subject matter of the course, "helping students value diversity and equity may influence students' acquisition of content knowledge" (Kitano, 1996, p. 29).

Unfortunately, Weinstein and Obear (1992) found that faculty members are wary of challenging biases in their classrooms for fear of doing so inadequately. Culturally inclusive practices, however, demand that rather than ignoring or minimizing such comments, we learn how to respond calmly and with compassion, regardless of the course topic.

Czopp, Monteith, and Mark (2006) found that those participants in their study who were confronted on their overt racial discrimination were more likely to feel guilty and uncomfortable about their own actions, two emotions that are crucial motivators of attitude and behavior adjustment. In fact, in follow-up studies, those participants who were confronted were subsequently less likely to display bias both in their actions and in their attitudes compared with those who were not challenged on their biases. Moreover, Czopp (2007) found that bystanders who witnessed a successful confrontation of discrimination were themselves more likely to challenge bias when they witnessed it, something that could be considered a pay-it-forward scenario. Clearly, challenging bias can be an effective approach, not only for the microaggressor, but also for the bystanders who observe the confrontation.

Many obstacles stand in the way, however, of acting upon an offensive comment or behavior. Sometimes it takes time to process the fact that a comment could be construed as offensive, and the conversation proceeds before it can be pointed out. Some people choose not to challenge a comment because they consider the risk too great; specifically, they are concerned with how they will be perceived and/or how their relationships may be affected. Some feel that any efforts on their part are inconsequential to the larger problems of discrimination (Ashburn-Nardo, Morris, & Goodwin, 2008).

Many people are inexperienced with challenging offensive comments and so do not know how to respond or are unable to respond in the heat of the moment. Plous (2000) found several responses that are not likely to produce negative repercussions such as resentment or opposition. Four suggestions are: (1) responding with a question (e.g., "Can you please help me understand how you came to that conclusion about a whole group of people?"); (2) reminding microaggressors of their self-perception as being fair-minded (e.g., "You always seemed like a person who respected equality and social differences, so I'm surprised to hear you say that"); (3) making it personal (e.g., "I feel uncomfortable when I hear you say that"); and (4) working to avoid smugness (e.g., "Because of all the stereotypes in society, I understand why you might think that, but you might consider thinking differently"). It is important to consider various scenarios before they occur; practice can be quite valuable in terms of preparing ourselves for these inevitable confrontations (Ashburn-Nardo, Morris, & Goodwin, 2008).

Multicultural competence is context-dependent. There's no one right answer for every situation that will be successful in every situation. It depends on the situation, the willingness of the other person to engage, our eagerness to listen rather than to critique, and our ability to figure out where they are coming from so we can meet them at that juncture and have a dialogue, rather than a monologue (Offermann & Phan, 2002).

Boysen and Vogel (2009) suggest that ignoring bias in the classroom implies complicity. Thus, they argue that any response is better than no response at all. They also recommend that we assess our interventions of bias in the classroom to see how students perceive the success of the intervention. This could be done via solicitation of an anonymous response from students, which can serve two purposes. First, it gives us valuable insight into how we can respond in the future; and second, it lets the students know that we believe challenging bias effectively is an important part of our role in the classroom, so much so that we are working to continuously improve our effectiveness. The impact of following up can be just as great as the response to the offensive comment or behavior.

TRANSFORMING SELF-AWARENESS

Reacting to offensive comments is not simply a matter of course, where a comment is made and we just respond. These comments are typically fraught with an emotional charge. Thus, responding effectively depends in large part on our ability to recognize and acknowledge our own emotional reactions.

Emotional intelligence, or EI (Goleman, 1995), is used primarily in leadership development with the idea that recognizing and understanding our own and others' emotional states is conducive to better leadership practices. EI mandates that we go through a process of self-discovery. If educators are self-aware about our own emotions, we are more likely to manage those emotions successfully, especially in times of stress. In other words, not only is it important to manage the emotions of students in the classroom as the sensitive topics of gender, race, sexuality, and so on come up—which they do, no matter what subject is being taught—but also, as the facilitator of the class, we need to be aware of our own *triggers:* those topics that bring about a physiological and, thus, an emotional response in us.

EI has been essential to my work in the classroom. For example, before I knew about EI, when I would hear an offensive comment coming from one of my students, my first reaction was frustration, anger, and a resultant fast heartbeat. I would probably become a bit red in the face and I wanted to verbally react without thinking. When I began to learn more about EI, I found that instead of reacting, my goal was to be aware of my emotions. Simply admitting to myself that I was being triggered was a big step toward a productive outcome. It reminded me that despite the fact that I might have a desire to lash out, an aggressive or defensive response from the instructor could be demoralizing and destructive. It could produce lasting consequences not only for the student who made the offending comment, but also for the rest of the class in terms of their future willingness to participate.

Acknowledging my trigger allowed me the chance to take a deep breath and remember that students, like everyone in society, have been socialized to believe misinformation. Whatever comment was spoken simply represented this lack of knowledge, and said very little about the instigator. I could then gently challenge the comment in a calm, compassionate, effective way by letting the perpetrator and those who heard the comment know that I was troubled by the language use/comment/behavior, regardless of the intention. It would give me the opportunity to unpack the process of microaggressions: that it is not the intent that matters, but the impact of the underlying message.

Possessing self-awareness about our own triggers allows us to calm down in the face of challenging moments and respond without causing the perpetrator to become defensive. Actually, self-awareness is useful before we even get into such a situation, first, to acknowledge that we do, in fact, have triggers; second, to consider what they are; and third, to play out a scenario in our mind to practice how we might react constructively. I have far fewer triggers in the classroom than I used to because of this process. In addition, understanding our own triggers helps us to be more compassionate when we witness other people experiencing a trigger.

Further, self-awareness in a broader context has been shown to increase intercultural awareness and sensitivity (Brown, 2004a). Self-awareness or "self-concept" includes processing our own experiences and behaviors, reflecting on our thought processes, and accepting ourselves as we are (Bandura, 1986; Ryan, 1992). Brown (2004a) elucidates, "Self-concepts are lenses through which beliefs, motivations, and behaviors are filtered" (p. 123) to make sense of our experiences, resolve internal discrepancies, regulate our behaviors, and adapt our expectations. Going through this process of self-discovery to have a better idea of who we are and how we act in various situations is correlated with inclusive behavior toward students and the ability to foster academic excellence (Allinder, 1994; Novick, 1996; Phuntsog, 1999; Tschannen-Moran & Hoy, 2001).

Ortiz and Patton (2012) explain, "Self-awareness is not simply about the self, but . . . the self in relation to others. . . . [I]dentity and one's awareness of identity is learned through social interactions that not only identify who you *are*, but also, who you *are not*" (p. 14). We tend to evaluate others based on our own beliefs and values (Varner, 2001). If someone else's values are dissimilar from our own, or if they don't meet our own standards, they are often perceived as deficient. Understanding our own perceptions and their limitations allows us to grasp the scope of the viewpoints and experiences of which we are not aware, with a sense of humility and sensitivity. We can challenge ourselves to increase our perspective taking by experiencing a wide variety of philosophies, ideas, literature, and so forth (Avery & Thomas, 2004). As we continue to self-assess what we know, the misperceptions we have learned, and what we still need to learn, we open up to the possibilities and benefits inherent in applying culturally inclusive practices.

TRANSFORMING OUR LANGUAGE

Our language use tells us a lot about who we are, where we come from, and what our biases and prejudices are. Language is a powerful tool in shaping our view of reality; it constructs meaning for us depending on how it is used. Language is the way we interact with one another and the means by which we perpetuate oppression and privilege in society as well as in our own personal relationships (Samuels, 2009b).

One example is how male privilege is created and perpetuated by language use. Even today, Richardson (2002) argues, most grammar books stipulate that the pronoun *he* can be used as a generic form of *he* or *she*. Many contend that it simply does not matter that we use the word *man* as generic for humans because everyone knows we mean humans, and not specifically men. However, Richardson (2002) points out:

> Research has consistently demonstrated that when the generic *man* is used, people visualize men, not women. . . . Man, then, suggests not humanity but rather

> male images. . . . One consequence is the exclusion of women in the visualization, imagination, and thought of males and females. (p. 510)

Richardson highlights the fact that this male-dominated language use has grave implications for the career aspirations of all genders. For example, if young students hear the word *policeman* as opposed to *police officer*, they will likely imagine a male in their minds. If female students hear *policeman*, they are much less likely to make a personal connection to this career path, resulting in the belief that only males can grow up to be police officers. This disconnect contributes to a self-fulfilling prophecy—in fact, the U.S. Department of Justice reports that the majority of police officers (80%) are still men (Langton, 2010). Richardson (2002) further points out that we tend to use *he* when referring to high-status jobs (doctor, lawyer, judge) and *she* when referring to lower-status jobs (nurse, secretary).

Eliminating Biased Language

There are several avenues to eliminating language bias. One would be to use gender-neutral plural words such as *they*. Further, we can use gender-neutral words such as *individual* or *person*, instead of *man;* and we can substitute the term *first-year student* for *freshman*, or *humanity* for *mankind*. We can also challenge the status quo by referring to a person in a high-status position using the *she* pronoun (e.g., "as the leader, she . . .").

In a male-identified society, one might ask, what does it matter? Why make such a big deal about language when there are bigger issues to tackle? Rothenberg (2000) answers this question with a provocation against the historic use of *he/him*. She suggests, "If the use of the pronoun is so inconsequential, we might as well use 'she' and 'her' instead of 'he' and 'him' for the next several hundred years" (p. 118). It is unlikely that undermining the precedent of using masculine pronouns would be a satisfactory solution in our patriarchal society.

Understanding Cultural Differences of Language

The language we use to talk about people can shape the way we view, interact, and behave toward them. For example, just as race is socially constructed, so too is disability. Who is considered disabled has changed over time and varies across cultures (Linton, 1998). For example, who has been labeled intellectually disabled based on IQ scores has changed over time, and has resulted in severe social and political consequences. Further, different cultures perceive disability differently. For example, war-torn countries tend to have many more people who have been wounded; typically, those countries tend to normalize disability in ways that other countries have not (L. Ware, personal communication, October 23, 2013).

When we think about disability, the language used is most often rooted in the standard of a temporarily nondisabled body, and is based on what a person can't (or can no longer) do. This is known as a deficit model and this way of thinking (and speaking) about a disabled person can be considered offensive. Linton (1998) writes that the goal is to see people with disabilities "as whole, purposeful, sentient people" rather than seeing a person with impaired vision, for example, as defined only by their disability, focusing on "unsteadiness, darkness, limited vision, sadness, ineptness, the absence of light and enlightenment, and any number of other substitutions for the real experience of women and men with disabilities" (p. 127). The deficit model is reductive; it problematizes disability, strips the humanity from people with disabilities, and encourages well-meaning, temporarily nondisabled people to treat those with disabilities as deprived, unfortunate, or pitiable.

If our point of departure, on the other hand, is the culturally inclusive approach of seeing all people as whole, then we can also acknowledge that it is not people who are disabled, but rather it is the culture that disables them by limiting access to buildings, bathrooms, and a choice of where to sit in a classroom, among other things. That said, *disability* is currently considered respectful language, an acknowledgment of the landmark legal decisions the disabled community has won in recent decades (L. Ware, personal communication, October 23, 2013).

How language is used can even make a difference in how we frame problems and, consequently, how and where we look for solutions. For decades, educational institutions, policymakers, educators, and even activists have been striving to close what they refer to as the "achievement gap." They have used this term to describe the difference in academic success between White students and students of color—most often, African American students. Framing this divergence in the context of the unfavorable results of underachieving students, we are, in a sense, blaming the victims of an unfair system. Instead, using the term *opportunity gap* transfers our focus from the results to the pervasive and persistent structural and environmental influences to this problem (Carter & Welner, 2013; Gorski, 2013).

Students with marginalized identities (students of color, students in poverty, and so on) "are not reaching their full potential and are not 'closing the gap' in achievement—precisely because they are not receiving equitable and meaningful opportunities to reach that potential" (Carter & Welner, 2013, p. 3). If we only look at educational inequities as gaps in achievement, our solutions will focus on outcomes only (such as high-stakes testing), rather than considering structural inputs such as equal access and providing the resources and support needed for all students to succeed (Carter & Welner, 2013).

How we use language in the classroom can have serious consequences for our students. Because our language acquisition and use is likely rooted in our cultural norms, and because most teachers are from dominant groups, we may unintentionally judge students based on dominant norms. Without the awareness of language rules and norms in other cultures, we may forfeit the chance for the student to accurately demonstrate knowledge.

For example, based on her analysis of language use, sociolinguist Carmen Fought (2006) considers one rule that varies by culture: what kind of information is acceptable to share. In some African American communities, children are discouraged from disclosing personal information. Thus, when a teacher's personal questions are met with silence because the student had been taught not to respond, the teacher might evaluate the student harshly, and might even label the student as uncooperative or difficult.

Another example is cultural differences in answering already-known/obvious answers (Heath, 1982). A teacher might start teaching about a topic by asking basic questions. In some African American communities, questions that have obvious answers—such as to describe the color or shape of something—simply would not be asked. The elapsed time it takes for a student from such a community to reorient and figure out what is being asked is enough to make the teacher question the student's learning capacity, when that time in actuality is a result of cultural differences and certainly is not a measure of the student's intelligence. Instead, it actually demonstrates an ability to reflect on, analyze, and quickly respond to a disorienting dilemma. Leap (1993) suggests that a similar situation exists with Native American students who are taught to value silence, especially when they are faced with new knowledge. Judging students by dominant values of when it is acceptable or even required to speak devalues the cultural knowledge they bring to the classroom.

How are these cultural differences influencing the way students are judged? It is no wonder that the dropout rate for such students is much greater than that for White students, because they have been dissuaded through dominant culture from considering themselves potential scholars. As Native American communities tend to value cooperation over competition and group harmony over conflict, many Native American students favor working in groups and dislike being singled out to answer a question. What values are we instilling in our students as we challenge them to fight for grades? As Fought (2006) points out, working cooperatively, learning by watching and doing, being allowed to make mistakes, and learning from one another seem to be values worth pursuing, not just for Native American students, but for all students.

TRANSFORMING OUR PRACTICES

Do we engage with our students in an inclusive manner? Culturally inclusive practices take forethought not only about our specific social identities, but also about our pedagogical techniques. Before we even step into a classroom, we can consider the ways in which certain identities are cued based on images displayed, verbal and nonverbal language use, cultural examples, and so forth (Steele, 2010). For example, as LGBTQ-friendly educators, we:

- don't assume that everyone is heterosexual;
- use inclusive language (e.g., *partner* or *someone special* rather than *boyfriend* or *girlfriend*);
- invite students to share their PGP (Preferred Gender Pronoun: *he, she, ze, they, and so on*);
- actively pursue our own education on LGBTQ issues, history, and current events, including gaining an understanding of the coming-out process;
- acknowledge and take responsibility for our own socialization, prejudice, and privilege;
- educate others on LGBTQ issues;
- challenge homophobia when it arises;
- acquire and provide resources when needed (from national, local, and campus organizations);
- include LGBTQ books and videos in the office, library, and/or classroom;
- understand the difference between sexuality and gender identity/expression;
- are aware that many LGBTQ community members are not inclined to report harassment of any kind;
- recruit and hire "out" LGBTQ employees; and
- make it clear to all that we are an LGBTQ ally (Safe Zone Training Manual, 2013).

The last suggestion serves not only to provide support for LGBTQ students, faculty, and staff, but also sends a positive model to other potential allies. The fact that this nonexhaustive list of inclusive practices is specific to only one social group demonstrates the magnitude of the challenge of becoming a culturally inclusive educator. The time and effort, however, are well worthwhile.

Challenges to Inclusiveness

Many students convey that in other classes, when they get to an issue about race (slavery, for example), everyone in the class turns to the one African American student in the class to see their reaction. In fact, students mention that it is often the teacher in the class who turns to one specific student to get "the African American perspective" or "the Asian perspective," or "the Hispanic perspective." This puts students who might already feel targeted in a classroom (where they might be the only student of color) in an uncomfortable position. It is not the responsibility of students of color to educate others about their race or their race's collective history. Further, White teachers and White students never seem to ask a White student for "the White perspective."

Inclusive educators make sure that students know that no one should be required or expected to speak for their whole race, gender, sexuality, disability, and so forth . . . students couldn't do so even if they wanted to! This provides all students, especially students of color, the opportunity to participate with the knowledge that they are speaking only from their own experience, regardless of the subject matter being taught.

Another challenge that potentially inclusive educators face is confusion about the difference between the concepts of equality and equity. While equality suggests that we treat every student the same, equity tends to refer to justice or fairness, taking the context and circumstances of an individual into account (Corson, 2001). The difference between these notions is not insignificant. If we are aspiring to equality, it may mean that we are striving to see all students objectively without their backgrounds, social identities, and lived experiences *getting in the way*. Unfortunately, equality also connotes oppression-blindness.

It is typically out of the mouths of White people that we hear the words, "I don't see color; we're all the same." First of all, most of us do, in fact, see color (unless we are medically colorblind). The fact that we're pretending we don't see color is a microaggression. As previously mentioned, colorblindness is not the answer to inequality; rather, it is a form of racism. Second, this *sameness* ideology does not represent the experiences of most people of color; they know that in most situations, they are not likely to be treated the same way, and with the same respect, as White people. Third, when we say that we are all the same, the question becomes. We are all the same *as who?* Typically, the answer is: the same as White people. This view not only whitewashes people of color into expectations of dominant culture, but also virtually ignores and excludes the wealth of knowledge, experience, and innovation that comes from diversity.

On the contrary, equity signifies an appropriate response to differences. McGee Banks and Banks (1995) explain that the pedagogy of equity includes multicultural education that should foster learning and attainment of the attitudes and skills necessary to become thoughtful, engaged members of a democratic society. Equity takes social differences and the social structure of inequality into account rather than assuming that we all begin on a level playing field and if we just worked hard enough, anyone could succeed. Adhering to equity pedagogy paves the way for teaching standards that are more just and more likely to lead to the success of the most students.

Strategies for Inclusiveness

Zeichner (1992) summarizes the broad range of literature that describes effective teaching strategies for inclusiveness. Among many approaches suggested are maintaining and communicating high standards for all students with the expectation that all students can succeed, believing that we can make a difference in students' learning and dedicating ourselves to attaining equity for all students, and building strong relationships with students rather than perceiving them as the *other*.

Considering inclusive practices more generally, my colleague Christina Jiménez and I created a broader list for educators who seek to become culturally inclusive. As inclusive educators, we:

- are reflective and vigilant about our own behavior every day with the knowledge that we can make a difference;
- acknowledge when we respond well and/or handle a situation well;
- recognize that unlearning oppressive beliefs and actions is a lifelong process, and welcome each learning opportunity;
- acknowledge and accept that we may not know how to handle every situation;
- ask for help when we need to, cultivating support from other inclusive educators;
- take responsibility for learning about our own and other group's heritage, culture, and experience;
- always assume that racism/sexism/heterosexism/and so on are part of the picture;
- are knowledgeable, comfortable, and proud of our own identities;
- listen to and respect the perspectives and experiences of the members of traditionally marginalized groups;
- are willing to take risks, try new behaviors, and act in spite of our own fears and resistance from others;

- take care of ourselves in order to avoid burnout;
- act against social injustice out of a belief that it is in our own self-interest to do so and with a willingness to make mistakes, learn from them, and try again;
- are willing to be confronted about our own behavior and attitudes, and consider change;
- understand the connections among all forms of social injustice;
- address issues, not just incidents; and
- are visible, active, vigilant, and public (even when a traditionally marginalized group member is not in the room). (Adams, Bell, & Griffin, 1997; Kivel, 2002; Wong (Lau), 2007)

Practicing inclusiveness is just that: a practice. It means acting with knowledge and intention to promote equity every chance we get, and taking responsibility for the consequences of our actions when our good intentions have led us astray of our purpose. It means living in congruence with our beliefs so that our actions are aligned with our goal of creating the world we hope to live in: one in which all members feel like they belong.

Chapter 7

Culturally Inclusive Leadership

> In the end we will conserve only what we love; we will love only what we understand; and we will understand only what we have been taught.
>
> —*Baba Dioum*

> The teacher is of course an artist, but being an artist does not mean that he or she can make the profile, can shape the students. What the educator does in teaching is to make it possible for the students to become themselves.
>
> —*Paulo Freire*

In an inclusiveness workshop I was facilitating for a group of faculty and staff at a military institution a few years back, I was surprised by the reactions I was receiving to what I considered basic ideas about exclusion. We were discussing the idea that we live in a patriarchal culture that advantages men over women (and I didn't even mention people who identify as transgender because the military was still operating under the policy of "Don't Ask, Don't Tell"). The resistance to the information we were discussing was palpable. It was so vehement, in fact (especially from high-ranking officers), that I felt as though I were being verbally attacked. The argument many of them were trying to make was that we are all equal now—especially in the military. Even female officers were making this argument, which affirmed that they, too, had bought into this oppressive myth.

This led me to ask myself many questions about the experience: First, why were these officers under the impression that all women, as they claimed, were treated equally in the military, especially in the wake of the sexual assault scandals that have occurred at many U.S. military institutions and academies? Second, why were they protecting the myth of gender equity so desperately? Third, why did they think that it was acceptable to behave the way they were behaving toward someone whom they had invited to their organization? Finally, what did this say about the leadership of the organization?

Although there were some kind officers who actually apologized afterward for the behavior of the entire group, most did not. We cannot view the group's behavior in a vacuum. This was not the intention of a few individuals who had been misinformed or who were simply exclusionary in their thoughts and actions. On the contrary, the situation spoke volumes about the oppressive attitudes and behaviors that were taken for granted in the organization and were unlikely ever challenged.

INCLUSIVE LEADERSHIP

This type of unjust governance is rooted in a historic view that leadership is supposed to be authoritarian. Ignoring or bulldozing over issues of cultural inclusion created a legacy of exclusion that was so pervasive that even the members of marginalized communities believed in the myths they were being fed. In today's growing multicultural society, a paradigm shift must be taken by those in leadership positions. A domineering ruler or ruling body is counterproductive to the mission of empowerment and engagement. In order to be prepared for the future—and to prepare our students—administrators and leaders of all kinds must embrace inclusive leadership.

One of the main foci of inclusive leadership is to challenge exclusive ideas and behaviors, create policy around social justice, and implement those policies through inclusive practices (Ryan, 2006). Most important, it is critical for all leaders to model those inclusive behaviors. In my work as a social justice educator of many years, I view leadership as more than simply based on one's rank in a specific organization. Like inclusiveness, leadership can be considered a verb. It is demonstrated by our words (both verbal and nonverbal) and actions that represent our values and the standards to which we hold ourselves accountable.

Practicing Leadership

Further, a commitment to diversity must come from both the top down and from the bottom up (Hurtado et al., 1998; Samuels & Samuels, 2003). In other words, although it is critical for the administration of an institution to create and maintain a commitment to diversity, it is also imperative that those involved in the everyday practices of that commitment be involved. Not only is leadership demonstrated when the chancellor of our university declared our campus to be "inclusive" and created the policies and practices to make our campus so, but it is also exhibited when a faculty member gently and openly challenges a student in the hallway who flippantly shouts,

"You retard" to another student. Leadership is when a 2nd-grade student holds the door open for the person behind them. Really, it is any behavior that other people can see and repeat. As educators, we must learn to behave in culturally inclusive ways so that we can invite others to participate, innovate, and build inclusivity.

One example of practicing inclusive leadership is in the determination and commitment displayed by the dean of the College of Education at Northern Illinois University, Dr. La Vonne Neal. She makes a habit of going into middle and high schools to encourage primarily disadvantaged students to excel and go to college. Often, she finds that they don't have any intention of going, but she walks into a classroom or an assembly and her first words are "Good morning, scholars!" This is the epitome of leadership. With this one practice, she empowers students to consider themselves capable of being academic superstars.

Retired basketball coach Phil Jackson (2013) talks about leading from the inside out. His goal was to get his players to lead and play using their own intuition, fostering confidence and trust in their courage to be authentic: "I always tried to foster an environment in which everyone played a leadership role, from the most unschooled rookie to the veteran superstar" (pp. 12–13). In his championship career, he brought meditation and mindfulness to his players so that they could learn to cultivate a single-pointed focus to their game and their lives. Building mental strength, he found, would be instrumental in developing strong relationships with teammates, another inclusive leadership skill. The relationships were so strong, in fact, that when one player erred on the court, the rest of the team would have his back. Informed by Zen principles, Jackson states, "I discovered that the more I tried to exert power directly, the less powerful I became. I learned to dial back my ego and distribute power as widely as possible." He adds, "Paradoxically, this approach strengthened my effectiveness because it freed me to focus on my job as keeper of the team's vision" (p. 12). This type of inclusive leadership lifts everyone up as Coach Jackson learned by leading his teams to championships 11 times! If we can take the lessons both from Dean Neal and Coach Jackson, we may find that reaching out and building relationships is the key to closing the opportunity gap and supporting every student, staff, and faculty member on any campus or in any school.

Implications of Faculty Unpreparedness

What are the implications of a faculty body whose members consider themselves already prepared to build cultural inclusiveness? How do we prepare educators to take on inclusive leadership practices? Through the research study in this book, which was conducted using rigorous methods, we now know more about faculty attitudes, intentions, and behaviors than ever before. The findings reveal that faculty members perceive themselves to be inclusive overall, yet they admit that they are less likely to practice inclusive behaviors. This substantiates the need to provide faculty members, and all educators, with education on how to behave inclusively.

Unfortunately, not only do we think we know how to be inclusive, but we also believe that we behave inclusively. And based on Social Desirability Theory, it is to our social benefit to consider ourselves inclusive because it has become more socially acceptable to be. At the same time, however, conversations around social identities are often downplayed and even silenced in society (e.g., even though the military's "Don't Ask, Don't Tell" policy around sexuality was overturned, discussing and getting support for transgender military students and officers remain taboo). When this happens, we are given the impression that race, gender, social class, sexuality, and so on don't matter. Even more than that, we receive the impression that we shouldn't focus on them so much. However, as long as inequalities exist, it is clear that social identities *do* matter because they are the basis on which those inequalities occur.

Worse still, if faculty members believe that they are already prepared to build cultural inclusiveness, then they may be less likely to take advantage of diversity and inclusiveness initiatives, even when these are offered. Clearly, more education is needed to teach educators to be on the lookout for and be willing to learn about and engage in what they don't know they don't know. Further, educators and administrators need to be open to feedback about the ways they engage with others. And we need to be assessing (and basing promotion on) how inclusive educators and administrators act in order to hold them accountable. Moreover, preparedness could have a strong impact on the recruitment and retention of diverse campus members, which remains a tremendous challenge on campuses and in schools across the United States.

Future Uses of the Survey Instrument

A campus or school that supports a diverse cultural environment can promote positive growth for all its members. One way to increase inclusive leadership on a campus or in a school is by educating faculty and staff members to create such an environment. Rooted in academic research and resources such as the Association of American Colleges and Universities (AACU), which details constructive inclusiveness strategies and techniques, the survey instrument created for the research in this book (see Appendix A) measures both attitudes and behaviors that are conducive to creating an inclusive atmosphere. The research has shed light on the extent to which

U.S. educators are prepared to build cultural inclusiveness, and in which areas they are more or less prepared (e.g., attitudes or behaviors). The survey instrument is unlike other tools that are currently available in three critical ways: (1) It incorporates theory and practice (praxis); (2) it is intersectional (bringing in issues of race, gender, class, sexuality, ability, and so forth); and (3) it incorporates the concept of privilege. Additionally, the survey instrument explores the extent to which educators have had prior education on diversity and inclusiveness. This survey instrument could be used as a tool for answering whether diversity is truly valued on a campus or in a school.

Despite an increase in diversity training in U.S. organizations and corporations, and the fact that, as mentioned above, substantial amounts of funds are allocated to such training, scholars agree that there is a dearth of rigorous assessment of these trainings (Hite & McDonald, 2006; Paluck, 2006; Pendry, Driscoll, and Field, 2007). The literature acknowledges that training is a salient feature of developing and maintaining an inclusive workplace, but more research is needed to understand and get the most out of training (Hite & McDonald, 2006). It is difficult to say whether the funding of diversity trainings has been worth the expense. Hence, the survey instrument in this research (see Appendix A) could also be used as a diversity initiative assessment tool. In other words, schools and campuses could use it as a pre- and posttest to evaluate the success of any programs they implement. The goal would be to see a positive change in staff and faculty members' preparedness for building campus or school inclusiveness. Interestingly, a positive change could mean that respondents realize that they are not as prepared as they originally thought they were, and understand the need and acquire the desire to learn more. The research in this book demonstrates that these concepts are quantifiable, and we can now pinpoint an individual's needs in terms of their strengths and challenges for building cultural inclusiveness.

Future iterations of the survey instrument (Appendix A) could be influential in the development of a national standard so that schools, colleges, and universities can evaluate how they are faring on their own campuses, and compare their findings with those of other campuses. The resulting scores would be useful to any potential students, faculty, and staff on any campus. In fact, the results could be used to help create policy in terms of funding faculty and staff development, which could impact recruitment and retention of diverse organizational members (Clewell & Ficklen, 1986).

Finally, many of the factors/sublatent constructs developed in the survey instrument are applicable to plenty of other kinds of respondents. Because this multidimensional survey includes perceptions, attitudes, and intentions of preparedness to build cultural inclusiveness, it could be tailored to P–12 teachers, staff, students, and members of other types of organizations, both nonprofit and corporate. The only sublatent construct that would need to be revised is Behavioral Outcomes, which would be different depending on the context of the organization and its members.

INCLUSIVE POLICIES FOR SUSTAINABLE CHANGE

The website for the Association of American Colleges and Universities' initiative on Making Excellence Inclusive states that the organization's purpose is to help colleges and universities "fully integrate their diversity and educational quality efforts and embed them into the core of academic mission and institutional functioning." This should be a key goal of every school, college, and university. Unfortunately, it is not yet. In the current economic downturn, it is critical for educational institutions to grow their markets in terms of recruitment and retention of diverse members. In a growing multicultural society, this is a sensible and positive step toward the future.

To do this, educational administrators should consider investing the time, effort, and funds necessary to create and maintain meaningful diversity programming for faculty and staff development. This is one solution to the financial challenges that most institutions are now facing. Even though the current economic condition could be used as an excuse not to engage in diversity initiatives, it is precisely because of these initiatives that educational institutions can stay afloat, demonstrating that diversity is truly valued on a campus and sending a strong message to all potential students, faculty, and staff. In fact, Alesina and La Ferrara (2005) suggest that diversity brings a multiplicity of abilities, experiences, and cultures that may lead to innovation and creativity. This could certainly have implications for new developments in, and varied sources of, funding.

As mentioned in Chapter 2, there is no national diversity policy for higher education currently in place and no national standard to measure how colleges and universities are doing in this area. If higher education is not mandated by a national body to create and sustain faculty development in the area of diversity as the National Council for Accreditation of Teacher Education (NCATE) is doing, it becomes incumbent on every college or university president to require this. It is also important to help faculty members become aware that they have self-efficacy in this area, and that they can act in inclusive ways to make a difference. As has been mentioned, this top-down, bottom-up approach can create sustainable change (Hurtado et al., 1998; Samuels & Samuels, 2003).

Scholars in the area of campus diversity suggest that thinking about increasing recruitment and retention of diverse school and campus members should be considered a process rather than an outcome. In fact, they discourage analysts from perceiving diversity as a box to be checked off a list, or only as a quantifiable number that is set as the ultimate goal. They recommend instead a multipronged approach such as recruitment of diverse students, faculty, and staff, building an encouraging campus climate, and transforming curriculum and research to reflect diversity and cultural inclusion (Milem et al., 2005). Arguably the leading national scholars on this topic, Hurtado et al. (1998) combined these concepts into two categories: representation and operations. In other words, they ask: "How diverse does the campus look in its representation of different cultural groups?" and "To what extent do campus operations demonstrate that racial and ethnic diversity is an essential value?" (p. 297). These two questions can be used to create a baseline for any educational institution in terms of how inclusive they are, and whether or not they practice inclusive leadership.

Faculty and staff development programs on inclusiveness leadership must be multidimensional and intersectional. Faculty should be asked to consider their own social group memberships and those of others. It might be useful for faculty development education to make use of current theoretical principles and to include examples of inclusive practices. This serves two purposes: (1) It can increase self-efficacy by demonstrating some of the often minor actions we can take to make a major impact, and (2) it can provide specific examples to which faculty members can connect and which perhaps they will remember the next time they are in a similar situation.

In addition, Chrobot-Mason (2003) suggests that inclusiveness training includes an individual action plan for change. The action plan can clarify projections and expectations for moving forward in this area, and can provide specific objectives and activities to achieve in a specific time frame. It is critical that all campus members take personal responsibility for increasing their multicultural aptitude and experiences. Doing so encourages ownership of the inclusiveness process, and therefore, a greater likelihood that action will, in fact, be taken (McKee & Schor, 1999).

In October 2009, Secretary of Education Arne Duncan spoke at the University of Virginia. In his speech, he stated, "Teaching should be one of our most revered professions, and teacher preparation programs should be among a university's most important responsibilities" (Duncan, 2009, para. 34). He also said:

> I believe that education is the civil rights issue of our generation. And if you care about promoting opportunity and reducing inequality, the classroom is the place to start. Great teaching is about so much more than education; it is a daily fight for social justice.

On January 5, 2010, the NCATE Panel on Clinical Preparation, Partnerships and Improved Student Learning met for the first time to make recommendations that will likely form the basis of changes to NCATE's accreditation standards in the future. James Cibulka, NCATE's president, stated that the panel will "identify what the best practices are in strong clinical preparation and in preparing teachers to more effectively teach diverse learners" (Epstein, 2010, para. 4).

These are strong indicators that changes in teacher preparation for inclusive leadership are on the way. If NCATE, which accredits more than 600 colleges and programs nationally, changes its accreditation practices to include teacher development on diversity issues, it is likely that P–12 teachers, at least, will be moving forward in this area. This is especially important in classrooms that are becoming more and more multicultural across the United States. Higher education must follow suit.

ARE WE READY?

The notion of teachers as role models and hands-on leaders has been around for at least a century in the writings of the educational reformer John Dewey. His pluralistic ideals put the responsibility for effective teaching and leadership in the hands of the educator rather than in one particular leader with a vision (Bogotch, 2000). Teaching as leadership is not based on random acts, but rather on a directed plan to heighten the learning of others (Murphy, Goldring, & Porter, 2006).

As the United States becomes more and more multicultural, how will we teach? How will we lead? What are we willing to do to become the most effective educational professionals we can be? And, most important, why? As leadership expert Simon Sinek (2009) points out in his book *Start with Why*, we will be much more successful and live more fulfilling, happier lives if we act from a place of "why" rather than "what" or "how." Knowing the "why" inspires us to lead more authentically and effectively. Sinek (2009) states, "Those who truly lead are able to create a following of people who act not because they were swayed, but because they were inspired." He adds, "Those who are able to inspire will create a following of people . . . who act for the good of the whole not because they have to, but because they want to" (pp. 7–8). In this light, as educational leaders, we have the opportunity to inspire those students, faculty, staff, and administrators with whom we come into contact every single day.

Leadership is hard work, as are all culturally inclusive practices. Dr. Heather Hackman suggests that we must take proper care of ourselves so that while we take on this challenging work, we can "bend but not break." She says that in order to preserve our strength over the long haul, it is important for us to figure out what our *anchors* are. Anchors are deeply felt values that come from within. One way to find yours is to "focus on a thought, memory, person, or experience that brings deep, heartfelt warmth in our hearts." Once we take a moment to do this, to really focus, we are able to ground ourselves and reenergize for the work ahead "so that we can continue to lean in and have hope" (personal communication, February 12, 2014).

In a growing multicultural world, there is so much to do to prepare for inclusive environments where students, educators, and staff can thrive. Although it is difficult to create systemic institutional change, we must remember that those systems and institutions are made up of individuals like us. We can create this change; we simply need to believe that we can and then acquire the skills to do so. We have so much power to effect change in every single interaction every single day. As William James said, "Act as if what you do makes a difference. It does." As we continue the lifelong process of becoming culturally inclusive educators, I challenge us to wake up, wake up, wake up, and heed his advice.

Survey Items

The actual survey included 15 additional items that were removed from the final version of the survey due to inadequate performance in the model. All items used a seven-point Likert scale: Strongly Disagree to Strongly Agree, unless otherwise specified.

1. In U.S. society, White people have certain unearned advantages that people of color do not receive.
2. In U.S. society, heterosexuals have certain unearned advantages that lesbian, gay, and bisexual people do not receive.
3. Discrimination against LGBT (lesbian, gay, bisexual, transgender) people is no longer a problem in the United States.*
4. In humans, homosexuality is just as natural as heterosexuality.
5. "Reverse discrimination" is a bigger problem than racism today.*
6. In general, transgender people (people whose self-identification challenges traditional notions of gender) should be accepted in society.
7. I am uncomfortable interacting with people on campus who are different from me in terms of their *race*.*
8. I am uncomfortable interacting with people on campus who are different from me in terms of their *gender*.*
9. I am uncomfortable interacting with people on campus who are different from me in terms of their *socioeconomic status*.*
10. I am uncomfortable interacting with people on campus who are different from me in terms of their *physical ability*.*
11. I am uncomfortable interacting with people on campus who are different from me in terms of their *age*.*
12. I am uncomfortable interacting with people on campus who are different from me in terms of their *religion/spirituality*.*
13. I consciously treat *female* campus members (students, faculty, and staff) with both respect and acceptance.

* Reverse coded

14. I consciously treat campus members (students, faculty, and staff) *of color* with both respect and acceptance.
15. I consciously treat *LGBT* campus members (students, faculty, and staff) with both respect and acceptance.
16. I consciously treat *non-Christian* campus members (students, faculty, and staff) with both respect and acceptance.
17. I consciously treat campus members (students, faculty, and staff) *with disabilities* with both respect and acceptance.

If campus inclusiveness refers to an environment that supports, represents, and welcomes members of diverse social groups, creating a culture where all members feel they belong.

18. It is my responsibility to make campus members (students, faculty, and staff) feel like they belong.
19. I have the skills to build inclusiveness on campus.
20. I can have an impact on campus inclusiveness.
21. I intend to build inclusiveness on campus.
22. The materials I use in my courses help students understand historical, social, and/or political events from diverse perspectives.
23. The texts/readings I use are written by authors from diverse backgrounds (different races, sexual orientations, genders, and so forth).
24. I draw references and examples from diverse cultural groups in my classes.
25. My students and I engage in meaningful dialogue about emotionally charged issues, such as discussions of race, religion, sexuality, and so on.
26. I enable students to demonstrate knowledge in multiple ways that reflect diverse learning styles.
27. I avoid dichotomizing issues of race into just Black and White, but instead incorporate diverse races (including multiracial issues) in my curriculum.
28. My institution provides meaningful education on diversity and inclusiveness for faculty and staff.**
29. Diversity and inclusiveness were an explicit part of my graduate education.**

** Items included as part of demographic information gathering

Research Methods and Analysis Procedures

RESEARCH METHODS

Sample

Institutions of higher education employ a total of 1.4 million faculty members, half of whom are full-time, the other half are part-time (Digest of Education Statistics, 2008). A random representative sample of 8,861 faculty members was pulled from a national mailing list and database management company. The sample was comprised of both part-time and full-time faculty members from all over the United States. These faculty members come from every kind of institution, including public, private, and military academies, in both 2-year and 4-year institutions. A total of 637 faculty members completed the emailed survey in its entirety, producing a response rate of approximately 7%. Of the sample, 84% identified as White, and 13.6% identified as people of color. Whites, therefore, were slightly overrepresented in this sample, as the national average is approximately 80%, and faculty of color were slightly underrepresented, as the national average is approximately 17% (U.S. Department of Education, 2009). Females comprised 49% of all respondents, which is higher than the national average of female faculty (42%). Males consisted of 41% of all respondents, which is lower than the national average of male faculty (58%) (U.S. Department of Education, 2007). There were 56 respondents (8.7%) who chose not to identify their gender, and 55 respondents (8.6%) who chose not to identify their race.

Analysis

Because the conceptual model for this research included a latent construct (i.e., faculty preparedness) made up of sublatent constructs, it was most appropriate to test this model using Structural Equation Modeling (SEM) (Bostic, Rubio, & Hood, 2000; Byrne, 2010; Kline, 1998; Noar, 2003; Schumacker & Lomax, 2004). The primary latent construct measured was *preparedness to build cultural inclusiveness*. The model proposed that the subconstructs of preparedness are perceptions of social inequality/attitudes about diversity, consideration of social group memberships, self-reflection of biases and behaviors, intention/self-efficacy, and inclusive behavioral outcomes.

The five factors were each made up of items that were on a seven-point Likert scale (Strongly Disagree to Strongly Agree). The first factor—perceptions of social inequalities/attitudes about diversity—was made up of six items. The second factor—consideration of social group memberships—also included six items. The third factor—self-reflection of biases—was comprised of five items, and the fourth factor—intention/self-efficacy—included four items. The fifth and final factor—behavioral outcomes—was made up of six items.

ANALYSIS PROCEDURES

To begin, the total sample (N = 637) was large enough to be randomly divided into two split-half samples for factor analysis (Comrey & Lee, 1992; Kass & Tinsley, 1979; Marsh, Balla, & McDonald, 1988; Tabachnick & Fidell, 2007). Using SPSS 17, half of the sample (n = 319) was used for an exploratory factor analysis (EFA) and the other half of the sample (n = 318) was used to confirm the findings of the EFA using confirmatory factor analysis (CFA). A hybrid Structural Equation Model (SEM) was then tested to evaluate both the validity of the measurement instrument and the proposed structural model.

After the sample was randomly split, basic demographics for each subsample were analyzed, as shown in Table B.1.

Exploratory Factor Analysis

Using SPSS, an EFA was conducted to determine any underlying structures for the variables in the model. The objective of EFA is also to retain the least number of factors while simultaneously explaining the most variance of the variables (Henson & Roberts, 2006). Principal axis factoring with direct oblimin rotation was conducted. Unconstrained, the procedure extracted five factors. The five extracted factors each had eigenvalues (or, the amount of total variance explained by each factor) greater than one, which is considered acceptable (Kaiser, 1960). Cumulatively, these five factors accounted for 60.8% of the variance. This initial version of the survey instrument (Appendix A) provides a modest attempt at explaining the underlying factors of faculty preparedness to build cultural inclusiveness.

The Kaiser-Meyer-Olkin (KMO) coefficient demonstrated excellent sampling adequacy at .85, suggesting the factor analysis should "yield distinct and reliable results" (Field, 2009, p. 647). Values above .70 are considered acceptable (Hutcheson

TABLE B.1. Demographics for the Randomly Split Samples

	EXPLORATORY FACTOR ANALYSIS SAMPLE (N = 319)		CONFIRMATORY FACTOR ANALYSIS SAMPLE (N = 318)	
Characteristic	Frequency	Percentage	Frequency	Percentage
Gender				
Male	140	43.9	150	47.2
Female	177	55.5	168	52.8
Transgender	1	.3	0	0
Race				
White	250	78.4	253	79.6
Faculty of Color	45	14.1	34	10.7
Sexual Orientation				
Heterosexual	287	90.0	277	87.1
LGBQ	23	7.2	22	6.9
Household Income				
Less than $40K	5	1.6	5	1.6
$40K–79K	82	25.7	86	27.0
$80K–120K	105	32.9	107	33.6
More than $120K	93	29.2	93	29.2
Age				
21–30	9	3.0	11	3.7
31–40	55	18.3	54	18.4
41–50	63	20.9	79	26.9
51–60	116	38.5	105	35.7
61+	58	19.3	45	15.3

& Sofroniou, 1999). Further, the Barlett's Test of Sphericity was significant ($\chi 2(351) = 5733.95$, $p < .000$), indicating that the correlations between variables were sufficiently large, further supporting the notion that factors do, in fact, exist within the data, and that factor analysis is appropriate to interpret the data (Field, 2009).

Next, internal consistency reliability was assessed using coefficient alphas (Cronbach, 1951). After those items with low factor loadings (< .60 to be more stringent) and low communalities were eliminated, the 27 items presented in Appendix A remained. Reliability statistics resulted in Cronbach's alphas as follows: Perceptions of Inequality/Attitudes About Diversity ($\alpha = .86$), Consideration of Social Group Memberships ($\alpha = .85$), Self-Reflection of Biases ($\alpha = .96$), Intention/Self-Efficacy ($\alpha = .85$), and Behavioral Outcomes ($\alpha = .87$). Alphas greater than .70 are considered acceptable (Kline, 1998), and here, all scales produced alphas of .85 and greater. Thus, the strong internal reliability of each scale demonstrated that the survey items more than adequately explained each of the five underlying constructs of faculty preparedness to build cultural inclusiveness that they were intended to explain. These findings provided sufficient justification to proceed to the confirmatory factor analysis.

Confirmatory Factor Analysis

With the use of the second half of the randomly split sample, AMOS 17 (Analysis of Moment Structures) was implemented to conduct the CFA to test construct validity of the survey instrument against the sample data (Byrne, 2010; McInerney & Ali, 2006). All indicators loaded significantly on their respective factors ($p < .001$). Table B.2 provides the results of the exploratory factor analysis, including factor loadings, reliability statistics, the variance explained for each factor, and the factor loadings indicated by the confirmatory factor analysis.

Structural Component of the Model

Structural equation modeling was used to test the structural model depicted in Figure B.1. The model included five first-order factors made up of a total of 27 items, and one second-order factor: preparedness to build cultural inclusiveness. Goodness-of-fit statistics evaluate the extent to which the underlying variables in a model represent the latent construct by determining how well the gathered data fits to the proposed model (Byrne, 2010). In this case, the analysis measures how well the five sublatent constructs represent the underlying construct of preparedness to build cultural inclusiveness. By all goodness-of-fit measures as suggested by Hu and Bentler (1999), the initial model fit to the data fell within fair limits. As is common practice, modification indices were reviewed (Byrne, 2010). These indices suggested that model fit would be improved by correlating several error terms. Once these correlations were made, the goodness-of-fit indices did, in fact, improve, producing a

TABLE B.2. Factor Loadings and Reliability Statistics for Exploratory Factor Analysis with Direct Oblimin Rotation and Confirmatory Factor Analysis of Faculty Preparedness to Build Cultural Inclusiveness Scales

Factors		LOADINGS	
		EFA sample	CFA* sample
Factor 1: Perceptions of Inequality/Attitudes About Diversity (α = .86, eigenvalue = 5.88, variance explained = 21.8%)			
Q1	In U.S. society, White people have certain unearned advantages that people of color do not receive.	.76	.55
Q2	In U.S. society, heterosexuals have certain unearned advantages that lesbian, gay, and bisexual people do not receive.	.80	.76
Q3	Discrimination against LGBT people is no longer a problem in the United States.[1]	.79	.83
Q4	In humans, homosexuality is just as natural as heterosexuality.	.69	.62
Q6	"Reverse discrimination" is a bigger problem than racism today.[1]	.66	.59
Q8	In general, transgender people should be accepted in society.	.66	.54
Factor 2: Consideration of Social Group Memberships (α = .85, eigenvalue = 3.64, variance explained = 13.5%)			
I am uncomfortable interacting with people on campus who are different from me in terms of their . . .			
Q52	Race.[1]	.81	.68
Q53	Gender.[1]	.67	.54
Q55	Socioeconomic Status.[1]	.74	.69
Q56	Physical Ability.[1]	.64	.57
Q57	Age.[1]	.74	.67
Q58	Religion/Spirituality.[1]	.65	.47
Factor 3: Self-Reflection of Biases (α = .96, eigenvalue = 3.11, variance explained = 11.5%)			
Q13	I consciously treat female campus members with both respect and acceptance.	.87	.91
Q14	I consciously treat campus members of color with both respect and acceptance.	.98	.97

TABLE B.2. Continued

Q15	I consciously treat LBGT campus members with both respect and acceptance.	.88	.87
Q16	I consciously treat non-Christian campus members with both respect and acceptance.	.94	.93
Q17	I consciously treat campus members with disabilities with both respect and acceptance.	.94	.92
Factor 4: Intention/Self-Efficacy (α = .86, eigenvalue = 2.54, variance explained = 9.4%)			
Q19	It is my responsibility to make campus members feel like they belong.	.66	.62
Q20	I have the skills to build inclusiveness on campus.	.79	.80
Q21	I can have an impact on campus inclusiveness.	.84	.82
Q22	I intend to build inclusiveness on campus.	.78	.82
Factor 5: Behavioral Outcomes (α = .89, eigenvalue = 1.26, variance explained = 4.7%)			
Q30	The materials I use in my courses help students understand historical, social, and/or political events from diverse perspectives.	.80	.77
Q31	The texts/readings I use are written by authors from diverse backgrounds.	.68	.66
Q32	I draw references and examples from diverse cultural groups in my classes.	.81	.82
Q33	My students and I engage in meaningful dialogue about emotionally charged issues, such as discussions of race, religion, sexuality, and so forth.	.74	.72
Q34	I enable students to demonstrate knowledge in multiple ways that reflect diverse learning styles.	.63	.55
Q35	I avoid dichotomizing issues of race into just Black and White, but instead incorporate diverse races (including multiracial issues) in my curriculum.	.75	.77

*Standardized Regression Weights

1. Reverse-coded item

FIGURE B.1. Structural Equation Model of Preparedness to Build Cultural Inclusiveness

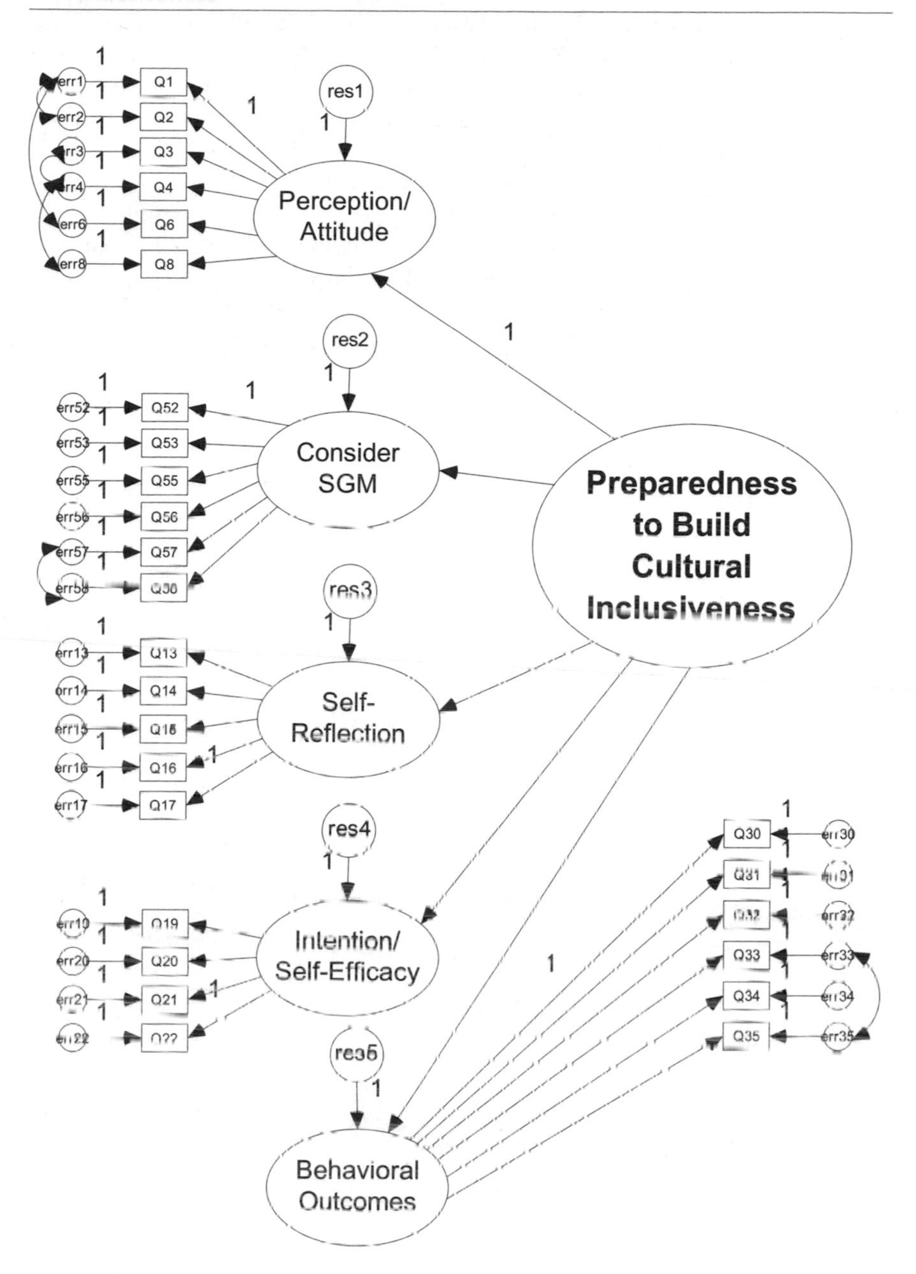

good fit to the data. (See Figure B.1 for a depiction of the final model.) That is, $\chi 2$ = 602.134; df = 313, $p < .000$; Root mean square error of approximation (RMSEA) = .05; RMSEA 90% CI ranged from .047 to .060. Standardized root mean squared residual (SRMR) = .069; comparative fit index (CFI) = .94; and the goodness-of-fit index (GFI) = .88. Hu and Bentler (1999) suggested that a well-fitting model would be indicated by an RMSEA of .05. They also found the use of a combinational rule wherein RMSEA > .05 (or .06) and SRMR > .06 (or .07), which is the case here, resulted in acceptable Type II error rates. If a CFI value > .9 suggests a good fit, then the value of .94, once again, indicates a good fit.

Additionally, the loadings for the five factors on preparedness to build cultural inclusiveness were as follows: Perceptions of Inequality/Attitudes About Diversity was .39, Consideration of Social Group Memberships was .45, Self-Reflection of Biases was .31, Intention/Self-Efficacy was .87, and Behavioral Outcomes was .66.

References

Aberson, C. L., Shoemaker, C., & Tomolillo, C. (2004). Implicit bias and contact: The role of interethnic friendships. *The Journal of Social Psychology, 144*(3), 335–347.

Adams, M., Bell, L. A., & Griffin, P. (Eds.). (1997). *Teaching for diversity and social justice: A sourcebook*. New York, NY: Routledge.

Ajzen, I., & Fishbein, M. (1977). Attitude-behavior relations: A theoretical analysis and review of empirical research. *Psychological Bulletin, 84*(5), 888–918.

Alesina, A., & La Ferrara, E. (2005). Preferences for Redistribution in the Land of Opportunities. *Journal of Public Economics, 89*(5), 897–931.

Allen, B. J. (2004). *Difference matters: Communicating social identity.* Long Grove, IL: Waveland Press.

Allen, B. J. (2005). Social constructionism. In S. May & D. K. Mumby, (Eds.), *Engaging organizational communication: Theory and research* (pp. 35–53). Thousand Oaks, CA: Sage Publications, Inc.

Allinder, R. M. (1994). The relationship between efficacy and the instructional practices of special education teachers and consultants. *Teacher Education and Special Education, 17,* 86–95.

Allport, G. W. (1979). *The nature of prejudice* (25th ed.). Reading, MA: Addison-Wesley.

Altman, H. B., & Cashin, W. E. (1992). *Writing a syllabus* (Idea Paper No. 27). Manhattan, KS: Kansas State University, Division of Continuing Education, Center for Faculty Evaluation and Development

Anand, R., & Winters, M. (2008). A retrospective view of corporate diversity training from 1964 to the present. *Academy of Management Learning & Education, 7*(3), 356–372.

Anti-Defamation League. (2005). *Master training manual.* New York, NY. Anti Defamation League Training and Curriculum Department.

Arminio, J., Torres, V., & Pope, R. (2012). Integrating student affairs values with the elements of inclusion. In J. Arminio, V. Torres, & R. L. Pope (Eds.), *Why aren't we there yet? Taking personal responsibility for creating an inclusive campus* (pp. 187–193). Sterling, VA: Stylus Publishing.

Aronson, E. (1978). *The jigsaw classroom.* Beverly Hills, CA: Sage.

Arredondo, P. (1996). *Successful diversity management initiatives.* Thousand Oaks, CA: Sage.

Ashburn-Nardo, L., Morris, K. A., & Goodwin, S. A. (2008). The confronting prejudiced responses (CPR) model: Applying CPR in organizations. *Academy of Management Learning & Education,* 7(3), 332–342.

Atkinson, D., Morten, G., & Sue, D. (1983). *Counseling American minorities: A cross-cultural perspective*. Dubuque, IA: William C. Brown.

Avery, D. R., & Thomas, K. M. (2004). Blending content and contact: The roles of diversity curriculum and campus heterogeneity in fostering diversity management competency. *Academy of Management Learning & Education, 3*(4), 380–396.

Banaji, M. R., & Greenwald, A. G. (2013). *Blindspot: Hidden biases of good people*. New York, NY: Delacorte Press.

Bandura, A. (1986). *Social foundations of thought and action: A social cognitive theory*. Englewood Cliffs, NJ: Prentice Hall.

Bandura, A. (2001). Social cognitive theory: An agentic perspective. *Annual Review of Psychology, 52*, 1–26.

Banks, J. A. (1995). Multicultural education: Historical development, dimensions, and practice. In J. A. Banks & C. A. McGee Banks (Eds.), *Handbook of research on multicultural education* (pp. 3–24). New York, NY: Simon & Schuster, Inc.

Barry, N. H., & Lechner, J. V. (1995). Preservice teachers' attitudes about and awareness of multicultural teaching and learning. *Teaching & Teacher Education, 11*(2), 149–161.

Becker, A. H., & Calhoon, S. K. (1999). What introductory psychology students attend to on a course syllabus. *Teaching Of Psychology, 26*(1), 6.

Bell, L. A. (1997). Theoretical foundations for social justice education. In M. Adams, L. A. Bell, & P. Griffin (Eds.), *Teaching for diversity and social justice: A sourcebook* (pp. 3–15). New York, NY: Routledge.

Bendick, M., Jr., Egan, M. L., & Lofhjelm, S. M. (2001). Workforce diversity training: From anti-discrimination compliance to organizational development. *Human Resource Planning, 24*(2), 10–25.

Bennett, C. (1995). *Comprehensive multicultural education: Theory and practice* (3rd ed.). Needham Heights, MA: Allyn & Bacon.

Bennett, M. J. (1986). A developmental approach to training for intercultural sensitivity. *International Journal of Intercultural Relations, 10*(2), 179–195.

Bensimon, E. (2005). Closing the achievement gap in higher education: An organizational learning perspective. *New Directions for Higher Education, 131*, 99–111.

Bensimon, E., & Malcolm, L. (Eds.). (2012). *Confronting equity issues on campus: Implementing the equity scorecard in theory and practice*. Sterling, VA: Stylus Publishing.

Bezrukova, K., Jehn, K. A., & Spell, C. S. (2012). Reviewing diversity training: Where we have been and where we should go. *Academy of Management Learning & Education, 11*(2), 207–227.

Black, P., & Wiliam, D. (1998). Inside the blackbox: Raising standards through classroom assessment. *Phi Delta Kappan, 80*, 139–148.

Blair, I. V., Ma, J. E., & Lenton, A. P. (2001). Imagining stereotypes away: The moderation of implicit stereotypes through mental imagery. *Journal of Personality and Social Psychology, 81*, 828–841.

Blasi, G. (2001). Advocacy against the stereotype: Lessons from cognitive social psychology. *UCLA Law Review*, *49*, 1241.

Bloom, A. (1987). *The closing of the American mind: How higher education has failed democracy and impoverished the souls of today's students.* New York, NY: Simon & Schuster, Inc.

Bluemel, A. (2011). *Looking for a relationship between diversity training and an inclusive company culture.* (Unpublished thesis). Carlson School of Management, University of Minnesota.

Bodenhausen, G. V., & Macrae, C. N. (1994). Coherence versus ambivalence in cognitive representations of persons. In R. S. Wyer, Jr. (Ed.), *Advances in social cognition* (Vol. 7, pp. 149–156). Mahwah, NJ: Lawrence Erlbaum Associates.

Bogotch, I. (2000). Educational leadership and social justice: Theory into practice. Paper Presented at the Meeting of the University Council for Educational Administration (UCEA), Albuquerque, NM.

Bolger, N., Zuckerman, A., & Kessler, R. C. (2000). Invisible support and adjustment to stress. *Journal of Personality and Social Psychology, 79,* 953–961.

Bonilla-Silva, E. (2003). *Racism without racists: Color-blind racism and the persistence of racial inequality in the United States.* Lanham, MD: Rowman & Littlefield.

Bonilla-Silva, E. (2009). Racism without "racists." In A. Ferber, C. M. Jiménez, A. O'Reilly Herrera, & D. R. Samuels (Eds.), *The matrix reader: Examining the dynamics of oppression and privilege* (pp. 176–181). New York, NY: McGraw-Hill.

Bostic, T. J., Rubio, D. M., & Hood, M. (2000) A validation of the subjective vitality scale using structural equation modeling. *Social Indicators Research, 52,* 313–324.

Boyle-Baise, M., & Sleeter, C. E. (1996). Field experiences: Planting seeds and pulling weeds. In C. Grant & M. Gomez (Eds.), *Making schooling multicultural: Campus and classroom* (pp. 371–388). Englewood Cliffs, NJ: Prentice Hall.

Boysen, G. A., & Vogel, D. L. (2009). Bias in the classroom: Types, frequencies, and responses. *Teaching of Psychology, 36*(1), 12–17.

Brewer, M. B., & Pierce, K. P. (2005). Social identity complexity and outgroup tolerance. *Personality and Social Psychology Bulletin, 31,* 428–437.

Bronson, P., & Merryman, A. (2009, September 14). See baby discriminate. *Newsweek.* Retrieved from www.newsweek.com

Brown, A. L. (1992). Design experiments: Theoretical and methodological challenges in creating complex interventions in classroom settings. *The Journal of the Learning Sciences,* 2(2), 141–178.

Brown, A. L., & Campione, J. C. (2002). Communities of learning and thinking, or a context by any other name. *Human Development, 21,* 108–125.

Brown, B. (2012). *Daring greatly: How the courage to be vulnerable transforms the way we live, love, parent, and lead.* New York, NY: Gotham Books.

Brown, E. L. (2004a) The relationship of self-concepts to changes in cultural diversity awareness: Implications for urban teacher educators. *The Urban Review,* *36*(2), 119–145.

Brown, E. L. (2004b). What precipitates change in cultural diversity awareness during a multicultural course: The message or the method? *Journal of Teacher Education, 55*(4), 325–340.

Brown, K. M. (2004). Leadership for social justice and equity: Weaving a transformative framework and pedagogy. *Educational Administration Quarterly, 40*(1), 77–108.

Bryan, C. J., Walton, G. M., Rogers, T., & Dweck, C. S. (2011). Motivating voter turnout by invoking the self. *Proceedings of the National Academy of Sciences, 108*(31), 12653–12656.

Burr, V. (2003). *Social constructionism.* New York, NY: Routledge.

Byrne, B. M. (2010). *Structural equation modeling with AMOS: Basic concepts, applications, and programming* (2nd ed.). New York, NY: Routledge.

Cameron, S. V., & Heckman, J. J. (2001). The dynamics of educational attainment for black, Hispanic, and white males. *Journal of Political Economy, 109*(3), 455-499.

Carter, D. J., & Wilson, R. (1994). *Twelfth annual status report on minorities in higher education.* Washington, DC: American Council on Education, Office of Minorities in Higher Education.

Carter, P. L., & Welner, K. G. (2013). Achievement gaps arise from opportunity gaps. In P. L. Carter & K. G. Welner (Eds.), *Closing the opportunity gap: What America must do to give every child an even chance* (pp. 1–10). New York, NY: Oxford University Press.

Chall, J. S. (2000). *The academic achievement challenge: What really works in the classroom.* New York, NY: Guilford.

Chang, M. J. (2002). The impact of an undergraduate diversity course requirement on students' racial views and attitudes. *The Journal of General Education, 51*(1), 21–42.

Cherryholmes, C. H. (1988). An exploration of meaning and the dialogue between textbooks and teaching. *Journal of Curriculum Studies, 20*(1), 1–21.

Chickering, A. W., & Gamson, Z. F. (1987). Seven principles for good practice in undergraduate education. *AAHE Bulletin, 39*(7), 3–7.

Chickering, A. W., & Gamson, Z. F. (1999). Development and adaptations of the seven principles for good practice in undergraduate education. *New Directions for Teaching and Learning, 80*, 75–81.

Chrobot-Mason, D. (2003). Developing multicultural competence for managers: Same old leadership skills or something new? *The Psychologist-Manager Journal, 6*(2), 5–20.

Chrobot-Mason, D., & Leslie, J. B. (2012). The role of multicultural competence and emotional intelligence in managing diversity. *The Psychologist-Manager Journal, 15*, 219–236.

Chrobot-Mason, D., & Quiñones, M. A. (2002). Training for a diverse workplace. In K. Kraiger (Ed.), *Creating, implementing, and managing effective training and development* (pp. 117–159). San Francisco, CA: John Wiley & Sons.

Chrobot-Mason, D., & Ruderman, M. N. (2003). Leadership processes in a diverse work environment. In M. S. Stockdale & F. J. Crosby (Eds.), *The psychology and management of workplace diversity* (pp. 100–121). Oxford, England: Blackwell.

Cialdini, R. B., & Goldstein, N. J. (2004). Social influence: Compliance and conformity. *Annual Review of Psychology, 55,* 591–621.

Clewell, B., & Ficklen, M. (1986). *Improving minority retention in higher education: A search for effective institutional practices.* (Rep. No. ETS-RR-86-17). Princeton, NJ: Educational Testing Service. Retrieved from http://eric.ed.gov/ERICDocs/data/ericdocs2sql/content_storage_01/0000019b/80/1d/bd/65.pdf

Cochran-Smith, M. (1995a). Color blindness and basket making are not the answers: Confronting the dilemmas of race, culture, and language diversity in teacher education. *American Educational Research Journal, 32,* 493–522.

Cochran-Smith, M. (1995b). Uncertain allies: Understanding the boundaries of race and teaching. *Harvard Educational Review, 63,* 541–570.

Comrey, A. L., & Lee, H. B. (1992). *A first course in factor analysis* (2nd ed.). Mahwah, NJ: Lawrence Erlbaum Associates.

Corson, D. (2001). Ontario students as a means to a government's ends. *Our schools/Our selves, 10*(4), 55–77.

Cox, T., Jr. (1991). The multicultural organization. *Academy of Management Executive, 5,* 34–47.

Cox, T., Jr. (1993). *Cultural diversity in organizations: Theory, research and practices.* San Francisco, CA: Berrett-Koehler.

Cox, T., Jr., & Beale, R. L. (1997). *Developing competency to manage diversity.* San Francisco, CA: Berrett-Koehler.

Cranton, P. (1994). *Understanding and promoting transformative learning: A guide for educators and adults.* San Francisco, CA: Jossey-Bass.

Cranton, P. (1996). Types of group learning. *New directions for adult and continuing education, 71,* 25–32.

Crenshaw, K. W. (1991). Mapping the margins: Intersectionality, identity politics, and violence against women of color. *Stanford Law Review, 43*(6), 1241–1299.

Cronbach, L. J. (1951). Coefficient alpha and the internal structure of tests. *Psychometrika, 16,* 297–334.

Cropper, C. (1994). Teaching for different learning styles. *Gifted Child Today, 17*(5), 36–39.

Cross, Jr., W. E. (1978). The Thomas and Cross models of psychological nigrescence: A review. *Journal of Black Psychology, 5,* 13–31.

Crowne, D. P., & Marlowe, D. (1964). *The approval motive: Studies in evaluative dependence* (p. 27). New York: Wiley.

Cuban, L. (1993). *How teachers taught: Constancy and change in American classrooms, 1890–1990* (2nd ed.). New York, NY: Teachers College Press.

Czopp, A. M. (2007, January). *Ramifications of confrontation observation: Does witnessing others' prejudice-related confrontations influence behavior?* Poster presented at the Annual Meeting of the Society of Personality and Social Psychology, Memphis, TN.

Czopp, A. M., Monteith, M., & Mark, A. Y. (2006). Standing up for a change: Reducing bias through interpersonal confrontation. *Journal of Personality and Social Psychology, 90,* 784–803.

Darley, J. M., & Gross, P. H. (1983). A hypothesis-confirming bias in labeling effects. *Journal of Personality and Social Psychology, 44*(1), 20.

Davidson, A. R., & Jaccard, J. J. (1979). Variables that moderate the attitude-behavior relation: Results of a longitudinal study. *Journal of Personality and Social Psychology, 37*(8), 1364–1376.

Davies, P. G., Spencer, S. J., Quinn, D. M., & Gerhardstein, R. (2002). Consuming images: How television commercials that elicit stereotype threat can restrain women academically and professionally. *Personality and Social Psychology Bulletin, 28*(12), 1615–1628.

Davies, P. G., Spencer, S. J., & Steele, C. M. (2005). Clearing the air: Identity safety moderates the effects of stereotype threat on women's leadership aspirations. *Journal of Personality and Social Psychology, 88*(2), 276–287.

Davis, L. (2002). Racial diversity in higher education: Ingredients for success and failure. *Journal of Applied Behavioral Science, 38*, 137–155.

Day, R. (2007). Developing the multi-cultural organisation: Managing diversity or understanding differences? *Industrial and Commercial Training, 39*(4), 214–217.

Devine, P. G. (1989). Stereotypes and prejudice: Their automatic and controlled components. *Journal of Personality and Social Psychology, 56*(1), 5–18.

Devine, P. G. (2001). Implicit prejudice and stereotyping: How automatic are they? *Journal of Personality and Social Psychology, 81*(5), 757–759.

Digest of Education Statistics. (2008). *Introduction.* Retrieved from http://nces.ed.gov/programs/digest/d08/

Dirkx, J. M. (2006). Engaging emotions in adult learning: A Jungian perspective on emotion and transformative learning. In E. W. Taylor (Ed.), *Teaching for Change. New Directions for Adult and Continuing Education, 109*, 15–26. San Francisco, CA: Jossey-Bass.

Dixon, T. L., & Linz, D. (2000). Overrepresentation and underrepresentation of African Americans and Latinos as lawbreakers on television news. *Journal of Communication, 50*(2), 131–154.

Dobbin, F., & Kalev, A. (2007). *Kicking and screaming: Commitment and resistance in organizational diversity programs.* Paper presented at the American Psychological Association National Conference, San Francisco, CA.

Dobbin, F., Kalev, A., & Kelly, E. (2007). Diversity management in corporate America. *Contexts, 6*(4), 21–27.

Dovidio, J. F., & Gaertner, S. L. (1997). Affirmative action, unintentional racial biases, and intergroup relations. *Journal of Social Issues, 52*, 51–57.

Dovidio, J. F., Gaertner, S. L., Stewart, T. L., Esses, V. M., & Ten Vergert, M. (2004). From intervention to outcomes: Processes in the reduction of bias. In W. G. Stephan & P. Vogt (Eds.), *Education programs for improving intergroup relations: Theory, research, and practice* (pp. 243–265). New York, NY: Teachers College Press.

Drouin, M. A. (2010). Group-based formative summative assessment relates to improved student performance and satisfaction. *Teaching of Psychology, 37*(2), 114–118.

Ducharme, E., & Agne, R. (1989). Professors of education: Uneasy residents of academe. In R. Wisniewski & E. Ducharme (Eds.), *The professors of teaching: An inquiry* (pp. 67–86). Albany, NY: State University of New York Press.

Duncan, A. (2009). A call to teaching: Secretary Arne Duncan's remarks at the Rotunda at the University of Virginia. Retrieved from www2.ed.gov/news/speeches/2009/10/10092009.html

Dunn, R. S., & Dunn, K. J. (1979). Learning styles/teaching styles: Should they . . . can they . . . be matched? *Educational Leadership, 36*(4), 238–245.

Dunsmuir, L. (2013). Many Americans have no friends of another race: Poll. *Reuters*. Retrieved from www.reuters.com/article/2013/08/08/us-usa-poll-race-idUSBRE97704320130808

Dunton, B. C., & Fazio, R. H. (1997). An individual difference measure of motivation to control prejudiced reactions. *Personality and Social Psychology Bulletin, 23*, 316–326.

Dutton, J. E., Dukerich, J. M., & Harquail, C. V. (1994). Organizational images and member identification. *Administrative Science Quarterly, 39*, 239–263.

Edyburn, D. L. (2010). Would you recognize universal design for learning if you saw it? Ten propositions for new directions for the second decade of UDL. *Learning Disability Quarterly, 33*, 33–41.

Eiseley, L. (1969). *The unexpected universe*. Orlando, FL: Harcourt Brace & Company.

Ely, R. J. (2004). A field study of group diversity, participation in diversity education programs, and performance. *Journal of Organizational Behavior, 25*, 755–780.

Ely, R. J., & Thomas, D. A. (2001). Cultural diversity at work: The effects of diversity perspectives on work group processes and outcomes. *Administrative Science Quarterly, 46*, 229–273.

Epstein, J. (2010, January). *Making teaching a profession*. Retrieved from www.insidehighered.com/news/2010/01/05/teachers

Fenwick, L. T. (2013). Upending stereotypes about black students. *Education Week*. Retrieved from www.edweek.org/ew/articles/2013/10/09/07fenwick_ep.h33.html?qs=upending+stereotypes

Ferber, A. (2007). Whiteness studies and the erasure of gender. *Sociology Compass, 1*(1), 265–282.

Ferber, A., Jiménez, C. M., O'Reilly Herrera, A., & Samuels, D. R. (Eds.). (2009). *The matrix reader: Examining the dynamics of oppression and privilege*. New York, NY: McGraw-Hill.

Field, A. (2009). *Discovering statistics using SPSS* (3rd ed.). London: Sage Publications.

Fiske, S. T. (1989). Examining the role of intent: Toward understanding its role in stereotyping and prejudice. In J. S. Uleman & J. A. Bargh (Eds.), *Unintended thought* (pp. 253–286). New York, NY: Guilford.

Flores, A. (2007). Examining disparities in mathematics education: Achievement gap or opportunity gap? *The High School Journal, 91*(1), 29–42.

Fought, C. (2006). *Language and ethnicity: Key topics in sociolinguistics*. Cambridge, UK: Cambridge University Press.

Fox, J. A., Hatfield, J. P., & Collins, T. C. (2003). Developing the curriculum transformation and disability workshop model. *Curriculum Transformation and Disability: Implementing Universal Design in Higher Education*, 23–39.

Frankel, B. (2009, September/October). How employee-resource groups drive innovation and engagement. *DiversityInc*, 15–26.

Frankenberg, R. (1993). *White women, race matters: The social construction of whiteness*. Minneapolis, MN: University of Minnesota Press.

Franklin, A. J. (1999). Invisibility syndrome and racial identity development in psychotherapy and counseling African American men. *The Counseling Psychologist*, 27, 761–793.

Freire, P. (1993). *Pedagogy of the oppressed*. New York: Continuum.

Freire, P., & Macedo, D. P. (1995). A dialogue: Culture, language, race. *Harvard Educational Review, 65*, 377–402.

Fried, J. (1993). Bridging emotion and intellect: Classroom diversity in process. *College Teaching*, *41*(4), 123–128.

Futrell, M. H. (1999). The challenge of the 21st century: Developing a highly qualified cadre of teachers to teach our nation's diverse student population. *Journal of Negro Education, 68*(3), 318–334.

Futrell, M. H., Gomez, J., & Bedden, D. (2003). Teaching the children of a new America: The challenge of diversity. *Phi Delta Kappan, 84*(5), 381–385.

Galinsky, A. D., & Moskowitz, G. B. (2000). Perspective-taking: Decreasing stereotype expression, stereotype accessibility, and in-group favoritism. *Journal of Personality and Social Psychology, 78*, 708–724.

Gallagher, C. (2009). Color-blinded America or how the media and politics have made racism and racial inequality yesterday's social problem. In A. Ferber, C. M. Jiménez, A. O'Reilly Herrera, & D. R. Samuels (Eds.), *The matrix reader: Examining the dynamics of oppression and privilege* (pp. 548–551). New York, NY: McGraw-Hill.

Ganster, D. C., Hennessey, H. W., & Luthans, F. (1983). Social desirability response effects: Three alternative models. *Academy of Management Journal*, *26*(2), 321–331.

Gay, G. (1997). The relationship between multicultural and democratic education. *The Social Studies, 88*(1), 5–11.

Gay, G. (2000). *Culturally responsive teaching: Theory, research and practice*. New York, NY: Teachers College Press.

Glenn, E. N. (1999). The social construction and institutionalization of gender and race. In M. M. Ferree, J. Lorber, & B. B. Hess (Eds.), *Revisioning gender* (pp. 3–43). Walnut Creek, CA: AltaMira Press.

Gokhale, A. A. (1995). Collaborative learning enhances critical thinking. *Journal of Technology Education, 7*(1). Retrieved from scholar.lib.vt.edu/ejournals/JTE/v7n1/gokhale.jte-v7n1.html?ref=Sawos.Org

Goleman, D. (1995). *Emotional intelligence*. New York, NY: Bantam Books.

Gonzalez, J. A. (2010). Diversity change in organizations: A systemic, multilevel, and nonlinear process. *Journal of Applied Behavioral Science, 46*(2), 197–219.

Goodman, D. J. (2001). *Promoting diversity and social justice: Educating people from privileged groups*. Thousand Oaks, CA: Sage Publications.

Gorski, P. C. (n.d.). Stages of multicultural curriculum transformation. EdChange. Retrieved from www.edchange.org/multicultural/curriculum/steps.html

Gorski, P. C. (2010). Beyond celebrating diversity: Twenty things I can do to be a better multicultural educator. *EdChange*. Retrieved from www.edchange.org/handouts/20things.doc

Gorski, P. C. (2013). *Reaching and teaching students in poverty: Strategies for erasing the opportunity gap*. New York, NY: Teachers College Press.

Gould, S. J. (1996). *The mismeasure of man*. New York, NY: W. W. Norton & Company.

Grant, C., & Secada, W. (1990). Preparing teachers for diversity. In W. R. Houston, M. Haberman, & J. Sikula (Eds.), *Handbook of research on teacher education* (pp. 403–422). New York, NY: Macmillan.

Grasha, A. F., & Yangarber-Hicks, N. (2000). Integrating teaching styles and learning styles with instructional technology. *College Teaching, 48*(1), 2–11.

Greenwald, A. G., McGhee, D. E., & Schwartz, J. L. K. (1998). Measuring individual differences in implicit cognition: The Implicit Association Test. *Journal of Personality and Social Psychology, 74*, 1464–1480.

Grimm, G. K. (2000). *Preparation of Fox Valley Technical College faculty for multicultural education.* Unpublished doctoral dissertation, University of Wisconsin–Stout.

Hackman, H. W. (2008). Broadening the pathway to academic success: The critical intersection of Social Justice Education, Critical Multicultural Education, and Universal Instructional Design. *Pedagogy and student services for institutional transformation: Implementing universal design in higher education*, 25–48.

Hannum, W., & Briggs, L. (1982). How does instructional system design differ from traditional instruction? *Educational Technology, 22*(1), 9–14.

Hardiman, R., & Jackson, B. (1997). Conceptual foundations for social justice courses. In M. Adams, L. Bell, & P. Griffin (Eds.), *Teaching for diversity and social justice: A sourcebook* (pp. 16–29). New York, NY: Routledge.

Heath, S. B. (1982). Questioning at home and school: A comparative study. In G. Spindler (Ed.), *Doing the ethnography of schooling: Educational anthropology in action* (pp. 105–127). New York, NY: Holt, Rinehart, and Winston.

Helms, J. E. (1984). Toward a theoretical explanation of the effects of race on counseling: A Black and White model. *Counseling Psychologist, 12*, 153–165.

Helms, J. E. (1995). An update of Helms' White and people of color racial identity models. In J. G. Ponterotto, J. M. Casas, L. A. Suzuki, & C. M. Alexander (Eds.), *Handbook of multicultural counseling* (pp. 181–198). Thousand Oaks, CA: Sage Publications.

Henson, R. K., & Roberts, J. K. (2006). Use of exploratory factor analysis in published research: Common errors and some comment on improved practice. *Educational and Psychological Measurement, 66*(3), 393–416.

Herring, C. (2013, December 17). The business case for diversity in higher education. *Chicago Sun Times*. Retrieved from www.suntimes.com/news/otherviews/24437121-452/the-business-case-for-diversity-in-higher-education.html

Hersey, P., & Blanchard, K. (1969). *Management of organization behavior.* Englewood Cliffs, NJ: Prentice Hall.

Higbee, J. L., Chung, C. J., & Hsu, L. (2004). Enhancing the inclusiveness of first-year courses through Universal Design. In I. M. Duranczyk, J. L. Higbee, &

D. B. Lundell (Eds.), *Best practices for access and retention in higher education* (pp. 13–26). Minneapolis, MN: University of Minnesota, General College, Center for Research on Developmental Education and Urban Literacy.

Hill Collins, P. (1990). *Black feminist thought: Knowledge, consciousness, and the politics of empowerment*. London: Harper Collins.

Hite, L. M., & McDonald, K. S. (2006). Diversity training pitfalls and possibilities: An exploration of small and mid-size US organizations. *Human Resource Development International, 9*(3), 365–377.

Holladay, C. L., Knight, J. L., Paige, D. L., & Quiñones, M. A. (2003). The influence of framing on attitudes toward diversity training. *Human Resource Development Quarterly, 14*, 245–263.

Holladay, C. L., & Quiñones, M. A. (2008). The influence of training focus and trainer characteristics on diversity training effectiveness. *Academy of Management Learning and Education, 7*, 343–354.

Hollins, E. R., & Guzman, M. T. (2005). Research on preparing teachers for diverse populations. In M. Cochran-Smith & K. M. Zeichner (Eds.), *Studying teacher education: The report of the AERA panel on research and teacher education* (pp. 477–548). Mahwah, NJ: Lawrence Erlbaum Associates.

Hong, W.-P., & Youngs, P. (2008). Does high-stakes testing increase cultural capital among low-income and racial minority students? *Education Policy Analysis Archives, 16*(6), 1–18.

Howard, G. R. (1999). *We can't teach what we don't know*. New York, NY: Teachers College Press.

Hu, L., & Bentler, P. M. (1999). Cutoff criteria for fit indexes in covariance structure analysis: Conventional criteria versus new alternatives. *Structural Equation Modeling, 6*(1), 1–55.

Humm, D. G., & Humm, K. A. (1944). Validity of the Humm-Wadsworth temperament scale: With consideration of the effects of subjects' response-bias. *The Journal of Psychology, 18*(1), 55–64.

Hurtado, S. (1992). The campus racial climate: Contexts for conflict. *The Journal of Higher Education, 63*(5), 539–569.

Hurtado, S., Milem, J., Clayton-Pedersen, A., & Allen, W. (1998). Enhancing campus climates for racial/ethnic diversity: Educational policy and practice. *The Review of Higher Education, 21*(3), 279–302.

Hutcheson, G., & Sofroniou, N. (1999). *The multivariate social scientist*. London, England: Sage Publications.

Ivancevich, J. M., & Gilbert, J. A. (2000). Diversity management: Time for a new approach. *Public Personnel Management, 29*, 75–92.

Jackson, P. (2013). *Eleven rings: The soul of success*. New York, NY: Penguin Group.

Janik, D. S. (2005). *Unlock the genius within*. Lanham, MD: Rowman and Littlefield Education.

Jensen, R. (2009). White privilege shapes the U.S.: Affirmative action for whites is a fact of life. In A. Ferber, C. M. Jiménez, A. O'Reilly Herrera, & D. R. Samuels (Eds.), *The matrix reader: Examining the dynamics of oppression and privilege* (pp. 186–188). New York, NY: McGraw-Hill.

Johnson, A. G. (2006). *Privilege, power, and difference* (2nd ed.). NY: Mayfield.

Johnson-Bailey, J., & Alfred, M. (2006). Transformational teaching and the practices of black women adult educators. In E. W. Taylor (Ed.), *Fostering transformative learning in the classroom: Challenges and innovations. New directions in adult and continuing education, 109*. San Francisco, CA: Jossey-Bass.

Jones, J. (1997). *Prejudice and racism* (2nd ed.). New York, NY: McGraw-Hill.

Kabat-Zinn, J. (2013). Mindfulness-based interventions in medicine and psychiatry: What does it mean to be "mindfulness-based"? In A. Fraser (Ed.), *The healing power of meditation* (pp. 93–119). Boston, MA: Shambhala Publications.

Kaiser, H. F. (1960). The application of electronic computers to factor analysis. *Educational and Psychological Measurement, 20*, 141–151.

Kalev, A., Dobbin, F., & Kelly, E. (2006). Best practices or best guesses? Assessing the efficacy of corporate affirmative action and diversity policies. *American Sociological Review, 71*, 589–617.

Kass, R. A., & Tinsley, H. E. A. (1979). Factor analysis. *Journal of Leisure Research, 11*, 120–138.

Katie, B. (2002). *Loving what is: Four questions that can change your life*. New York, NY: Three Rivers Press.

Katz, J. H. (1977). The effects of a systematic training program on the attitudes and behaviors of white people. *International Journal of Intercultural Relations, 1*(1), 77–89.

Katz, P. A. (1983). Developmental foundations of gender and racial attitudes. In R. L. Leahy (Ed.), *The child's construction of social inequality* (pp. 41–78). Waltham, MA: Academic Press.

Kea, C. D., Trent, S. C., & Davis, C. P. (2002). African American student teachers' perceptions about preparedness to teach students from culturally and linguistically diverse backgrounds. *Multicultural Perspectives, 4*(1), 18–25.

Kea, C. D., & Utley, C. A. (1998). To teach me is to know me. *The Journal of Special Education, 32*(1), 44–47.

Kellough, J. E., & Naff, K. C. (2004). Responding to a wake-up call: An examination of federal agency diversity management programs. *Administration and Society, 36*, 62–90.

Kezar, A., & Lester, J. (2009). Supporting faculty grassroots leadership. *Research in Higher Education, 50*(7), 715–740.

Kiefer-Boyd, K., & Kraft, L. M. (2003). Inclusion policy in practice. *Art Education*, 46–53.

King, E. B., Gulick, L. M., & Avery, D. R. (2010). The divide between diversity training and diversity education: Integrating best practices. *Journal of Management Education, 34*(6), 891–906.

King-Sears, M. (2009). Universal design for learning: Technology and pedagogy. *Learning Disability Quarterly, 32*, 199–201.

Kirkham, S. R., Van Hofwegen, L., & Harwood, C. H. (2005). Narratives of social justice: Learning in innovative clinical settings. *International Journal of Nursing Education Scholarship, 2*(1), 1–14.

Kitano, M. K. (1996). What a course will look like after multicultural change. In A. I. Morey & M. K. Kitano (Eds.), *Multicultural course transformation in higher education: A broader truth* (pp. 18–34). San Francisco, CA: Pearson.

Kivel, P. (2002). *Uprooting racism.* Gabriola, British Columbia: New Society Publishers.

Kline, R. B. (1998). *Principles and practice of structural equation modeling.* New York, NY: Guilford.

Kohli, R. (2008). Breaking the cycle of racism in the classroom: Critical race reflections from future teachers of color. *Teacher Education Quarterly,* 177–188.

Kohn, A. (2000). *The schools our children deserve: Moving beyond traditional classrooms and tougher standards.* New York, NY: Houghton Mifflin Company.

Kottler, J. A., & Englar-Carlson, M. (2009). *Learning group leadership: An experiential approach.* Thousand Oaks, CA: Sage Publications.

Kozol, J. (2005). *The shame of the nation.* New York, NY: Crown Publishers.

Kunda, Z. (1999). *Social cognition: Making sense of people.* Cambridge, MA: MIT Press.

Ladson-Billings, G. J. (1999). Preparing teachers for diverse student populations: A critical race theory perspective. In A. Iran-Nejad & D. Pearson (Eds.), *Review of research in education* (pp. 211–248). Washington, DC: American Educational Research Association.

Ladson-Billings, G. J. (2005). Is the team all right? Diversity and teacher education. *Journal of Teacher Education, 56,* 229–234.

Ladson-Billings, G. J., & Tate, W. F., IV. (1995). Toward a critical theory of education. *Teachers College Record, 97,* 47–68.

Langton, L. (2010). *Women in Law Enforcement, 1987-2008.* US Department of Justice, Office of Justice Programs, Bureau of Justice Statistics.

Leap, W. (1993). *American Indian English.* Salt Lake City, UT: University of Utah Press.

Lehman, P. R. (1993). The emotional challenge of ethnic studies classes. *College Teaching, 40*(4), 134–137.

Lepore, L., & Brown, R. (1997). Category and stereotype activation: Is prejudice inevitable? *Journal of Personality & Social Psychology, 72,* 275–287.

Lewin, K. (1951). *Field theory in social science.* New York, NY: Harper.

Linton, S. (1998). *Claiming disability: Knowledge and identity.* New York, NY: New York University Press.

Lippi-Green, R. (2012). *English with an accent: Language, ideology, and discrimination in the United States.* New York, NY: Routledge.

Lockwood, N. R. (2007). Workplace diversity: Leveraging the power of difference for competitive advantage. In J. H. Munro (Ed.), *Organizational leadership* (pp. 134–147). Dubuque, IA: McGraw-Hill.

Loewen, J. W. (2007). *Lies my teacher told me: Everything your American history textbook got wrong.* New York, NY: Simon & Schuster.

Lorber, J. (1994). "Night to his day": The social construction of gender. *Paradoxes of Gender, 1,* 1–8.

Love, B. (2004). Brown plus 50 counter-storytelling: A critical race theory analysis of the "Majoritarian Achievement Gap" story. *Equity & Excellence in Education,37*(3), 227–246.

Madera, J. M. (2013). Best practices in diversity management in customer service organizations: An investigation of top companies cited by Diversity Inc. *Cornell Hospitality Quarterly, 54*(2), 124–135.

Mahoney, J. L., & Cairns, R. B. (1997). Do extracurricular activities protect against early school dropout? *Developmental Psychology, 33*, 241–253.

Malone, T. W., & Lepper, M. R. (1987). Making learning fun: A taxonomy of intrinsic motivations for learning. *Aptitude, learning, and instruction, 3*, 223–253.

Mannix, E. A., & Neale, M. A. (2006). What differences make a difference? The promise and reality of diverse teams in organizations. *Psychological Science in the Public Interest, 6*, 32–55.

Marcus, A., Mullins, L. C., Brackett, K. P., Tang, Z., Allen, A. M., & Pruett, D. W. (2003). Perceptions of racism on campus. *College Student Journal, 37*(4), 611–626.

Markus, H. R., Steele, C. M., & Steele, D. M. (2000). Colorblindness as a barrier to inclusion: Assimilation and non-immigrant minorities. *Daedalus, 129*, 233–259.

Marsh, H. W., Balla, J. R., & McDonald, R. P. (1988). Goodness-of-fit indexes in confirmatory factor analysis: The effect of sample size. *Psychological Bulletin, 103*, 391–410.

Martin, O., & Williams-Dixon, R. (1994). Overcoming social distance barriers: Pre-service teachers' perceptions of racial ethnic groups. *Journal of Instructional Psychology, 21*, 76–82.

Martin, R. J. (1991). The power to empower: Multicultural education for student-teachers. In C. E. Sleeter (Ed.), *Empowerment through multicultural education* (pp. 287–297). Albany, NY: State University of New York Press.

Massey, D. S., Charles, C. Z., Lundy, G., & Fischer, M. J. (2002). *The source of the river: The social origins of freshmen at America's selective colleges and universities*. Princeton, NJ: Princeton University Press.

McCauley, C., Wright, M., & Harris, M. E. (2000). Diversity workshops on campus: A survey of current practice at U.S. colleges and universities. *College Student Journal, 34*(1), 100–114.

McConnell, A. R., & Leibold, J. M. (2001). Relations among the Implicit Association Test, discriminatory behavior, and the explicit measures of racial attitudes. *Journal of Experimental Social Psychology, 37*, 435–442.

McCutcheon, G. (1982). What in the world is curriculum theory? *Theory into Practice, 21*(1), 18–22.

McDermott, P. C., Rothenberg, J. J., & Gormley, K. A. (1999). The impact of community and school practica on new urban teachers. *The Educational Forum, 63*(2), 180–185.

McDonald, M. A. (2005). The integration of social justice in teacher education: Dimensions of prospective teachers' opportunities to learn. *Journal of Teacher Education, 56*(5), 418–435.

McGee Banks, C. A., & Banks, J. A. (1995). Equity pedagogy: An essential component of multicultural education. *Theory into Practice, 34*(3), 152–158.

McGuire, D., & Bagher, M. (2010). Diversity training in organisations: An introduction. *Journal of European Industrial Training, 34*(6), 493–505.

McInerney, D. M., & Ali, J. (2006). Multidimensional and hierarchical assessment of school motivation: Cross-cultural validation. *Educational Psychology, 26*(6), 717–734.

McIntosh, P. (1988). White privilege and male privilege: A personal account of coming to see correspondences through work in women's studies. Excerpted from Working Paper 189, Wellesley College Center for Research on Women, Wellesley, MA.

McIntosh, P. (1990). Interactive phases of curricular and personal re-vision with regard to race. Working Paper No. 219, Wellesley College Center for Research on Women, Wellesley, MA.

McKee, A., & Schor, S. (1999). Confronting prejudice and stereotypes: A teaching model. *Performance Improvement Quarterly, 12,* 181–199.

McMackin, M. C., & Bukowiecki, E. M. (1997). A change in focus: Teaching diverse learners within an inclusive elementary school classroom. *Equity & Excellence in Education, 30*(1), 32–39.

Melnick, S. L., & Zeichner, K. M. (1998). Teacher education's responsibility to address diversity issues: Enhancing institutional capacity. *Theory into Practice, 37*(2), 88–95.

Mezirow, J. (1994). Understanding transformation theory. *Adult Education Quarterly, 44*(4), 222–232.

Mezirow, J. (1996). Contemporary paradigms of learning. *Adult Education Quarterly, 46,* 158–172.

Micklos, J., Jr. (2013). You belong here. *Teaching Tolerance, 45*. Retrieved from www.tolerance.org/magazine/number-45-fall-2013/you-belong-here?elq=8c25b1c32e744270966e5b7fa9d92c74&elqCampaignId=168

Milem, J. F. (1994). Attitude change in college students: Examining the effect of college peer groups and faculty normative groups. *Journal of Higher Education, 69*(2), 117–140.

Milem, J. F., Chang, M., & Antonio, A. (2005). *Making diversity work on campus: A research-based perspective. Making Excellence Inclusive* Series. Washington, DC: Association of American Colleges and Universities.

Milner, H. R., Flowers, L. A., Moore, E., Jr, Moore, J. L., III, & Flowers, T. A. (2003). Preservice teachers' awareness of multiculturalism and diversity. *High School Journal, 87*(1), 63–70.

Moore, J. (2005). Is higher education ready for transformative learning? A question explored in the study of sustainability. *Journal of Transformative Education, 3*(1), 76–91.

Moradi, B., & Miller, L. (2009). Attitudes of Iraq and Afghanistan war veterans toward gay and lesbian service members. *Armed Forces & Society, 20*(10), 1–23.

Moreno, J., Smith, D. G., Clayton-Pedersen, A., Parker, S., & Teraguchi, D. (2006). *The revolving door for underrepresented minority faculty in higher education: An analysis from the Campus Diversity Initiative.* Retrieved from www.irvine.org/assets/pdf/pubs/education/insight_Revolving_Door.pdf

Morris, L., Romero, J., & Tan, D. L. (1996). Changes in attitude after diversity training. *Training and Development, 50*(9), 54–55.

Murphy, J., Goldring, E., & Porter, A. (2006). *Leadership for learning: A research-based model and taxonomy of behaviors.* Wallace Foundation State Action for Educational Leadership Conference, St. Louis, MO.

National Collaborative on Diversity in the Teaching Force. (2004). *Assessment of diversity in America's teaching force: A call to action.* Washington, DC: National Collaborative on Diversity in the Teaching Force.

Neal, L. V., Webb-Johnson, G., & McCray, A. (2003). Movement matters: The need for culturally responsive teaching. *The Journal of the New England League of Middle Schools, 15*, 28–33.

Nguyen, H. D., & Ryan, A. M. (2008). Does stereotype threat affect test performance of minorities and women? A meta-analysis of experimental evidence. *Journal of Applied Psychology, 93*(6), 1314–1334.

Nieto, S. (1999). *The light in their eyes: Creating multicultural learning communities.* New York, NY: Teachers College Press.

Noar, S. M. (2003). The role of structural equation modeling in scale development. *Structural Equation Modeling, 10*(4), 622–647.

Norton, M. I., & Sommers, S. R. (2011). Whites see racism as a zero-sum game that they are now losing. *Perspectives on Psychological Science, 6*(3), 215–218.

Novick, R. (1996). *Developmentally appropriate and culturally responsive education: Theory and practice.* Portland, OR: Northwest Regional Educational Laboratory.

Nunnally, J. C. (1978). *Psychometric theory* (2nd ed.). NY: McGraw-Hill.

Oakes, J., Rogers, J., & Silver, D. (2004). *Separate and unequal 50 years after Brown: California's racial "opportunity gap."* Los Angeles: University of California, Los Angeles, Institute for Democracy, Education, and Access.

Obach, B. K. (1999). Demonstrating the social construction of race. *Teaching Sociology,* 27(3), 252–257.

Offermann, L. R., & Phan, L. U. (2002). Culturally intelligent leadership for a diverse world. In R. E. Riggio, S. E. Murphy, & F. J. Pirozzolo (Eds.), *Multiple intelligences and leadership* (pp. 187–214). Mahwah, NJ: Lawrence Erlbaum Associates.

Oliver, M. B. (2003). African American men as "criminal and dangerous": Implications of media portrayals of crime on the "criminalization" of African American men. *Journal of African American Studies,* 7(2), 3–18.

O'Malley, J., & McCraw, H. (1999). Students perceptions of distance learning, online learning and the traditional classroom. *Online Journal of Distance Learning Administration, II(IV).* Retrieved from www.westga.edu/~distance/ojdla/winter24/omalley24.html

Omi, M., & Winant, H. (2009). Racial formations. In A. Ferber, C. M. Jiménez, A. O'Reilly Herrera, & D. R. Samuels (Eds.), *The matrix reader: Examining the dynamics of oppression and privilege* (pp. 51–57). New York, NY: McGraw-Hill.

Ore, T. (Ed.). (2006). *The social construction of difference and inequality: Race, class, gender, and sexuality* (3rd ed.). New York, NY: McGraw-Hill.

Ortiz, A. M., & Patton, L. D. (2012). Awareness of self. In J. Arminio, V. Torres, & R. L. Pope (Eds.), *Why aren't we there yet? Taking personal responsibility for creating an inclusive campus* (pp. 9–31). Sterling, VA: Stylus Publishing.

Page, N., & Czuba, C. E. (1999). Empowerment: What is it? *Journal of Extension, 37*(5). Retrieved from http://joe.org/index.php

Paluck, E. L. (2006). Peer pressure against prejudice: A field experimental test of a national high school prejudice reduction program. Working Paper, Harvard University, Cambridge, MA.

Paluck, E. L., & Green, D. P. (2009). Prejudice reduction: What works? A review and assessment of research and practice. *Annual Review of Psychology, 60,* 339–367.

Parker, L., & Lynn, M. (2002). What's race got to do with it? Critical race theory's conflicts with and connections to qualitative research methodology and epistemology. *Qualitative Inquiry, 8*(1), 7–22.

Parker, P. (2009). For the white person who wants to know how to be my friend. In A. Ferber, C. M. Jiménez, A. O'Reilly Herrera, & D. R. Samuels (Eds.), *The matrix reader: Examining the dynamics of oppression and privilege* (p. 522). New York, NY: McGraw-Hill.

Parsad, B., Lewis, L., Westat, E. F., & Greene, B. (2001). *Teacher preparation and professional development: 2000.* Washington, DC.

Pendry, L. F., Driscoll, D. M., & Field, C. T. (2007). Diversity training: Putting theory into practice. *Journal of Occupational and Organizational Psychology, 80,* 27–50.

Peters, W. (Director). (1970). *Eye of the storm.* [Documentary]. ABC News: USA.

Pettigrew, T.F., & Tropp, L.R. (2006). A meta-analytic test of intergroup contact theory. *Journal of Personality and Social Psychology, 90,* 751–783.

Pettis-Renwick, W. (2002). From the margins to the center: Reconstructing the canon in social studies curriculum. In L. Darling-Hammond, J. French, & S. P. García-Lopez (Eds.), *Learning to teach for social justice* (pp. 30–38). New York, NY: Teachers College Press.

Phuntsog, N. (1999). The magic of culturally responsive pedagogy: In search of the genie's lamp in multicultural education. *Teacher Education Quarterly, 26,* 97–111.

Pierce, C. M. (1988). Stress in the workplace. In A. F. Coner-Edwards & J. Spurlock (Eds.), *Black families in crisis: The middle class* (pp. 27–34). New York, NY: Brunner/Mazel.

Plantenga, D. (2004). Gender, identity, and diversity: Learning from insights gained in transformative gender training. *Gender and Development, 12*(1), 40–46.

Plaut, V. C., Sanchez-Burks, J., Buffardi, L., & Stevens, F. G. (2007). *What about me? Understanding non-minority aversion to diversity initiatives in the workplace.* Unpublished manuscript, University of Georgia.

Plous, S. (2000). Responding to overt displays of prejudice: A role-playing exercise. *Teaching of Psychology, 27,* 198–200.

Powell, A. A., Branscombe, N. R., & Schmitt, M. T. (2005). Inequality as ingroup privilege or outgroup disadvantage: The impact of group focus on collective guilt and interracial attitudes. *Personality and Social Psychology Bulletin, 31,* 508–521.

Powell, J. A. (2012). *Racing to justice: Transforming our conceptions of self and other to build an inclusive society*. Bloomington, IN: Indiana University Press.

Ramirez, A., & Carpenter, D. (2005). Challenging assumptions about the achievement gap. *Phi Delta Kappan, 86*(8), 599–603.

Richardson, L. (2002). Gender stereotyping in the English language. In K. E. Rosenblum & T-M. Travis (Eds.), *The meaning of difference: American constructions of race, sex and gender, social class, and sexual orientation* (3rd ed., pp. 509–515). New York, NY: McGraw-Hill.

Richeson, J. A., & Nussbaum, R. J. (2004). The impact of multiculturalism versus color-blindness on racial bias. *Journal of Experimental Social Psychology, 40,* 417–423.

Roberson, L., Kulik, C. T., & Pepper, M. B. (2003). Using needs assessment to resolve controversies in diversity training design. *Group & Organization Management, 28*, 148–174.

Roberson, L., Kulik, C. T., & Tan, R. Y. (2013). Effective diversity training. *The Oxford handbook of diversity and work* (pp. 341–365).

Rothenberg, P. S. (2000). *Invisible privilege: A memoir about race, class, and gender.* Lawrence, KS: University Press of Kansas.

Rothenberg, P. S. (2009). *Race, class, and gender in the United States: An integrated study* (8th ed.). New York, NY: Worth Publishers.

Roy, L. (2013, November 18). Faculty diversity: We still have a lot to learn. *The Chronicle of Higher Education.* Retrieved from http://chronicle.com/article/Faculty-Diversity-Still-a-Lot/143095/

Russell-Brown, K. (1998). *The color of crime: Racial hoaxes, white fear, black protectionism, police harassment, and other macroaggressions.* New York, NY: NYU Press.

Ryan, J. (2006). *Inclusive leadership*. San Francisco, CA: John Wiley & Sons, Inc.

Ryan, K. (1992). The moral education of teachers. In K. Ryan & T. Lickona (Eds.), *Foundations of Moral Education: Vol. 3. Character Development in Schools and Beyond* (2nd ed., pp. 287–304). Washington, DC: Council for Research in Values and Philosophy.

Ryan, R. M., & Deci, E. L. (2000). Self-determination theory and the facilitation of intrinsic motivation, social development, and well-being. *American Psychologist, 55,* 68–78.

Rynes, S., & Rosen, B. (1995). A field survey of factors affecting the adoption and perceived success of diversity training. *Personnel Psychology, 48,* 247–270.

Sadker, M., & Sadker, D. (1995). *Failing at fairness.* New York, NY: Scribner.

Sadker, M., & Sadker, D. (2009). Missing in interaction. In T. Ore (Ed.), *The social construction of difference and inequality* (pp. 331–343). New York, NY: McGraw-Hill.

Safe Zone Training Manual. (2013). *NDSU Safe Zone Packet,* North Dakota State University. Retrieved from www.ndsu.edu/fileadmin/safezone/2012_2013_Safe_Zone_Packet.pdf

Salcedo, M. (2003). Faculty and the 21st century student in USA higher education. *Inroads—The SIGCSE Bulletin, 35*(2), 83–87.

Salisbury, M., & Goodman, K. (2009). Educational practices that foster intercultural competence. *Diversity & Democracy: Civic Learning for Shared Futures, 12*, 12–13.

Samuels, D. R. (2009a). Introduction to understanding oppression and privilege. In A. Ferber, C. M. Jiménez, A. O'Reilly Herrera, & D. R. Samuels (Eds.), *The matrix reader: Examining the dynamics of oppression and privilege* (pp. 139–145). New York, NY: McGraw-Hill.

Samuels, D. R. (2009b). Sounds and silences of language. In A. Ferber, C. M. Jiménez, A. O'Reilly Herrera, & D. R. Samuels (Eds.), *The matrix reader: Examining the dynamics of oppression and privilege* (pp. 502–507). New York, NY: McGraw-Hill.

Samuels, D. R. (2009c). *Teaching race, gender, class, and sexuality: A teaching guide to accompany The Matrix Reader*. New York, NY: McGraw-Hill.

Samuels, D. R. (2013a). On white privilege. *Stories on Diversity.* Beyond Diversity Resource Center. Retrieved from http://bdrcblogstories.wordpress.com/2013/07/28/

Samuels, D. R. (2013b). Social identity development and discordance in an intersectional diversity and inclusiveness workshop. *Understanding and Dismantling Privilege, 3*(1).

Samuels, S. M., & Samuels, D. R. (2003). Reconstructing culture: Privilege and change at the United States Air Force Academy. *Race, Gender, and Class: Special Edition on Privilege, 10*(4), 120–144.

Sanders, W. L. (1998). Value-added assessment. *The School Administrator, 55*(11), 24–27.

Sanders, W. L., & Horn, S. P. (1998). Research findings from the Tennessee Value-Added Assessment System (TVAAS) database: Implication for educational evaluation and research. *Journal of Personnel Evaluation in Education, 12*(3), 247–256.

Schmader, T., Johns, M., & Barquissau, M. (2004). The costs of accepting gender differences: The role of stereotype endorsement in women's experience in the math domain. *Sex Roles, 50*(11–12), 835–850.

Schneider, B., Martinez, S., & Owens, A. (2006). Barriers to educational opportunities for Hispanics in the United States. In M. Tienda & F. Mitchell (Eds.), *Hispanics and the future of America* (pp. 179–227). Washington, DC: National Academies Press.

Schneider, C. G. (2000). Diversity requirements. *Liberal Education, 86*(4), 2–5.

Schoorman, D. (2002). Increasing critical multicultural understanding via technology: "Teachable moment" in a university-school partnership project. *Journal of Teacher Education, 53*(4), 356–369.

Schuerholz-Lehr, S. (2007). Teaching for global literacy in higher education: How prepared are the educators? *Journal of Studies in International Education, 11*(2), 180–204.

Schugurensky, D. (2002). Transformative learning and transformative politics: The pedagogical dimension of participatory democracy and social action. *Expanding the Boundaries of Transformative Learning*, 59–76.

Schumacker, R. E., & Lomax, R. G. (2004). *A beginner's guide to structural equation modeling* (2nd ed.). Mahwah, NJ: Lawrence Erlbaum Associates.

Schunk, D. (1989). Self-efficacy and cognitive skill learning. In C. Ames & R. Ames (Eds.), *Research on motivation in education* (Vol. 3, pp. 13–44). San Diego, CA: Academic Press.

Schwartz, R. S. (2001). Racial profiling in medical research. *New England Journal of Medicine, 344*(18), 1392–1393.

Segal, M., & Martinez, T. (Eds.). (2007). *Intersections of gender, race, and class: Readings for a changing landscape*. Los Angeles, CA: Roxbury.

Sen, A. (1990). Individual freedom as a social commitment. In M. A. Wallis & S. Kwok (Eds.), *Daily struggles: The deepening racialization and feminization of poverty in Canada* (pp. 275–292). Ontario, Canada: Canadian Scholars' Press.

Shapiro, T., Meschede, T., & Osoro, S. (2013, February). *The roots of the widening racial wealth gap: Explaining the black-white economic divide.* (Research and Policy Brief). Waltham, MA: Institute on Assets and Social Policy.

Shotter, J. (1993). *Cultural politics of everyday life: Social constructionism, rhetoric and knowing of the third kind.* University of Toronto Press.

Silver, P., Bourke, A., & Strehorn, K. C. (1998). Universal instructional design in higher education: An approach for inclusion. *Equity & Excellence, 31*(2), 47–51.

Simons, T. (2002). Behavioral integrity: The perceived alignment between managers' words and deeds as a research focus. *Organization Science, 13,* 18–35.

Sinek, S. (2009). *Start with why: How great leaders inspire everyone to take action.* New York, NY: Penguin Group.

Skiba, R. J., Horner, R. H., Chung, C-G., Rausch, M. K., May, S. L., & Tobin, T. (2011). Race is not neutral: A national investigation of African American and Latino disproportionality in school discipline. *School Psychology Review, 40*(1), 85–107.

Sleeter, C. E., & Grant, C. A. (2010). Race, class, gender, and disability in current textbooks. In E. F. Provenzo, Jr., A. N. Shaver, & M. Bello (Eds.), *The textbook as discourse: Sociocultural dimensions of American schoolbooks* (pp. 183–215). New York, NY: Routledge.

Smedley, A., & Smedley, B. D. (2005). Race as biology is fiction, racism as a social problem is real: Anthropological and historical perspectives on the social construction of race. *American Psychologist, 60*(1), 16–26.

Sobel, D. M., Iceman-Sands, D., & Basile, C. (2007). Merging general and special education teacher preparation programs to create an inclusive program for diverse learners. *The New Educator, 3*(3), 241–262.

Sobel, D. M., & Taylor, S. V. (2005). Diversity preparedness in teacher education. *Kappa Delta Pi Record, 41*(2), 83–86.

Sobel, J. (2002). Can we trust social capital? *Journal of Economic Literature, 40,* 139–154.

Solórzano, D. (1998). Critical race theory, race and gender microaggressions, and the experience of Chicana and Chicano scholars. *International Journal of Qualitative Studies in Education, 11*(1), 121–136.

Solórzano, D., Ceja, M., & Yosso, T. (2000). Critical race theory, racial microaggressions, and campus racial climate: The experiences of African American college students. *Journal of Negro Education, 69,* 60–73.

Stanford Center for Opportunity Policy in Education and the National Education Policy Center. (2013). *Policy recommendations.* Retrieved from http://nepc.colorado.edu/sites/all/themes/fusion/fusion_starter/book/files/oppgappolicyrecs.pdf

Stangor, C. (Ed.). (2001). *Stereotypes and prejudice.* Philadelphia, PA: Psychology Press.

Steele, C. M. (2010). *Whistling Vivaldi and other clues to how stereotypes affect us.* New York, NY: W.W. Norton & Co.

Steele, C. M., & Aronson, J. (1995). Stereotype threat and the intellectual test performance of African Americans. *Journal of Personality and Social Psychology, 69*(5), 797–811. doi: 10.1037/0022-3514.69.5.797

Stevens, F. G., Plaut, V. C., & Sanchez-Burks, J. (2008). Unlocking the benefits of diversity: All-inclusive multiculturalism and positive organizational change. *Journal of Applied Behavioral Science, 44*(1), 116–133.

StosselClassroom. (2009). *Stereotypes – Stossel in the Classroom.* ABC News: USA. Retrieved from http://www.youtube.com/watch?v=ASDzcvyatgw

Stronks, K. (1997). Socio-economic inequalities in health: Individual choice or social circumstances? (Doctoral dissertation). Retrieved from http://publishing.eur.nl/ir/repub/asset/18068/stronk.pdf

Sue, D. W. (1981). *Counseling the culturally different.* New York, NY: John Wiley and Sons.

Sue, D. W. (2010). *Microaggressions in everyday life: Race, gender, and sexual orientation.* Hoboken, NJ: John Wiley & Sons.

Sue, D. W., Arredondo, P., & McDavis, R. J. (1992). Multicultural counseling competencies and standards: A call to the profession. *Journal of Counseling & Development, 70,* 477–486.

Sue, D. W., Capodilupo, C. M., & Holder, A. M. B. (2008). Racial microaggressions in the life experience of black Americans. *Professional Psychology: Research and Practice, 39*(3), 329–336.

Sue, D. W., Capodilupo, C. M., Torino, G. C., Bucceri, J. M., Holder, A. M., Nadal, K. L., & Esquilin, M. (2007). Racial microaggressions in everyday life: Implications for clinical practice. *American Psychologist, 62*(4), 271–286.

Swail, W., Redd, K., & Perna, L. (2003). Retaining minority students in higher education: A framework for success. *ASHE-ERIC Higher Education Report, 30*(2). Retrieved from http://66.102.1.104/scholar?hl=en&lr=&q=cache:lQgMtPT6BFcJ: www.studentretention.org/pdf/Swail_Retention_Book.pdf+higher+education+minority+retention

Swartz, E., & Bakari, R. (2005). Development of the teaching in urban schools scale. *Teaching and Teacher Education, 26,* 829–841.

Tabachnick, B. G., & Fidell, L. S. (2007). *Using multivariate statistics* (5th ed.). Boston, MA: Allyn & Bacon.

Tan, D., Morris, L., & Romero, J. (1996). Changes in attitude after diversity training. *Training & Development, 50*(9), 54–55.

Tatum, B. D. (2003). *Why are all the black kids sitting together in the cafeteria?* New York, NY: Basic Books.

Taylor, E. W. (1997). Building upon the theoretical debate: A critical review of the empirical studies of Mezirow's transformative learning theory. *Adult Education Quarterly, 48,* 34–60.

Taylor, E. (1998). A primer on critical race theory: Who are the critical race theorists and what are they saying? *Journal of Blacks in Higher Education, 19*(1), 122–124.

Taylor, E. W. (2008). Transformative learning theory. *New Directions for Adult and Continuing Education, 119*, 5–15.

Terrill, M. M., & Mark, D. L. (2000). Preservice teachers' expectations for schools with children of color and second-language learners. *Journal of Teacher Education, 51*(2), 149–155.

Thomas, K. M., & Plaut, V. C. (2008). The many faces of diversity in the workplace. In K. M. Thomas (Ed.), *Diversity resistance in organizations: Manifestations and solutions* (pp. 1–22). Mahwah, NJ: Lawrence Erlbaum.

Tschannen-Moran, M., & Hoy, A. W. (2001). Teacher efficacy: Capturing an elusive construct. *Teaching and teacher education, 17*(7), 783–805.

University of California v. Bakke, 438 U.S. 265 (1978).

U.S. Census Bureau. (2004). U.S. Interim projections by age, sex, race, and Hispanic origin. Retrieved from www.census.gov/population/www/projections/usinterimproj/

U.S. Census Bureau. (2012). National population projections. Retrieved from http://www.census.gov/population/projections/data/national/2012.html

U.S. Department of Education, National Center for Education Statistics. (2007). *Integrated Postsecondary Education Data System (IPEDS)*. Retrieved from http://nces.ed.gov/programs/digest/d08/tables/dt08_249.asp

U.S. Department of Education, National Center for Education Statistics. (2009). *Digest of Education Statistics, 2008* (NCES 2009-020), Table 246. Retrieved from http://nces.ed.gov/fastfacts/display.asp?id=61

van Dick, R., Wagner, U., Pettigrew, T. F., Christ, O., Wolf, C., Petzel, T., Castro, V. S., & Jackson, J. S. (2004). Role of perceived importance in intergroup contact. *Journal of Personality & Social Psychology, 87*(2), 211–227.

Van Ryn, M., & Fu, S. S. (2003). Paved with good intentions: Do public health and human service providers contribute to racial/ethnic disparities in health? *American Journal of Public Health, 93*(2), 248–255.

Varner, I. I. (2001). Teaching intercultural management communication: Where are we? Where do we go? *Business Communication Quarterly, 64*, 99–111.

Vittrup, B. (September 14, 2009). Even babies discriminate: A nurtureshock excerpt. *Newsweek*. Retrieved from http://www.newsweek.com/even-babies-discriminate-nurtureshock-excerpt-79233

Vygotsky, L. S. (1978). *Mind in society*. Cambridge, MA: MIT Press.

Wallace, J. M., Jr., Goodkind, S. G., Wallace, C. M., & Bachman, J. (2008). Racial/ethnic and gender differences in school discipline among American high school students: 1991–2005. *Negro Educational Review, 59*, 47–62.

Walton, G. M., & Cohen, G. L. (2007). A question of belonging: Race, social fit, and achievement. *Journal of Personality and Social Psychology, 92*(1), 82–96.

Ward, N. (2006). Improving equity and access for low-income and minority youth into institutions of higher education. *Urban Education, 41*, 50–70.

Wasonga, T. A. (2005). Multicultural education knowledgebase, attitudes and preparedness for diversity. *International Journal of Educational Management, 19*(1), 67–74.

Weinstein, G., & Obear, K. (1992). Bias issues in the classroom: Encounters with the teaching self. *New Directions for Teaching and Learning, 52,* 39–50.

Wentling, T., Schilt, K., Windsor, E., & Lucal, B. (2008). Teaching transgender. *Teaching Sociology, 36*(1), 49–57.

Wiggins, R. A., & Follo, E. J. (1999). Development of knowledge, attitudes, and commitment to teach diverse student populations. *Journal of Teacher Education, 50*(2), 94–105.

Williams, D. A., & Wade-Golden, K. C. (2007). The chief diversity officer. *College and University Professional Association for Human Resources, 59*(1), 38–47.

Wininger, S. R. (2005). Using your tests to teach: Formative summative assessment. *Teaching of Psychology, 32*(3), 164–166.

Wong (Lau), K. (2007). Building alliances among women of color and white women: Be an ally, not a friend. *On Campus with Women, 36*(1). Association of American Colleges and Universities. Retrieved from www.aacu.org/ocww/volume36_1/feature.cfm?section=2

Yang, Y., & Konrad, A. M. (2011). Understanding diversity management practices: Implications of institutional theory and resource-based theory. *Group & Organization Management, 36*(1), 6–38.

Zeichner, K. M. (1992). *Educating teachers for cultural diversity.* East Lansing, MI: National Center for Research on Teacher Learning.

Zeichner, K. M. (1993). Traditions of practice in U.S. pre-service teacher education programs. *Teaching and Teacher Education, 9,* 1–13.

Zeichner, K. M., & Hoeft, K. (1996). Teacher socialization for cultural diversity. In J. Sikula, T. J. Buttery, & E. Guyton (Eds.), *Handbook of research on teacher education* (2nd ed., pp. 525–547). New York, NY: Macmillan.

Zimbardo, P., & Ebbesen, E. (1970). *Influencing attitudes and changing behavior.* Reading, MA: Addison-Wesley.

Zinn, H. (2005). *A people's history of the United States: 1492 to present.* New York, NY: Harper Perennial Modern Classics.

Index

About the Author

Dena R. Samuels teaches in Women's and Ethnic Studies at the University of Colorado–Colorado Springs, and is the director of the Matrix Center for the Advancement of Social Equity and Inclusion. She provides seminars and consultation to schools, campuses, and organizations nationally and internationally on the processes of integrating diversity and building cultural inclusiveness.